FELIX
EXPLORES OUR
WORLD

Written by
Marc Tyler Nobleman

Illustrated by
George Ulrich

Based on characters created by
Annette Langen
and Constanza Droop

Special thanks to
Leslie Moseley

ABBEVILLE KIDS
A Division of Abbeville Publishing Group
New York · London

Dedicated to
Leslie Moseley and Dan Tucker
Sincere thanks to
Bob Abrams; Meredith Schizer; Patricia Fabricant; Jennifer Pierson; Samantha Trautman;
Erica Gordon; Rachel Loonin; Lisa Goldstein; Diana Frerking; Dorothy Gutterman;
Linda Coleman; David Le; the British, Swedish, Dutch, and Italian Consulates in Los Angeles;
the guys at Leon's Barber Shop in Los Angeles; and especially to Daniela.

EDITORS: Meredith Wolf and Jeffrey Golick
DESIGNERS: Jordana Abrams and Paula Winicur
PRODUCTION MANAGERS: Lou Bilka and Louise Kurtz
EDITORIAL ASSISTANT: Raegan Randolph

Original characters from *Letters from Felix, Felix Travels Back in Time, Felix Explores Planet Earth, Felix's Christmas Around the World, Felix: What Time Is It?* copyright © 1994, 1995, 1996, 1997, 1998 Coppenrath Verlag, Münster. Based on characters created by Annette Langen and Constanza Droop.

First edition
10 9 8 7 6 5 4 3 2 1

ISBN 0-7892-0596-3

Nobleman, Marc Tyler 1972-

Pages 63-65, 96, 97, 159, 168, 228, 233, 234, 236, 237 by Leslie Moseley

Thank you for picking up this book.

I have one quick question.

Do you like tests?

No?

Well . . .

Would you please take a very short one, for me, Felix? Please?

You don't want to, but you will anyway?

Thank you!

Ready?

Open this book to any page.

Read.

Look at the pictures.

See if you want to look at another page.

Yes?

You do?

Great!

You passed the test.

Easy test, right?

CONTENTS

CONTENTS (continued)

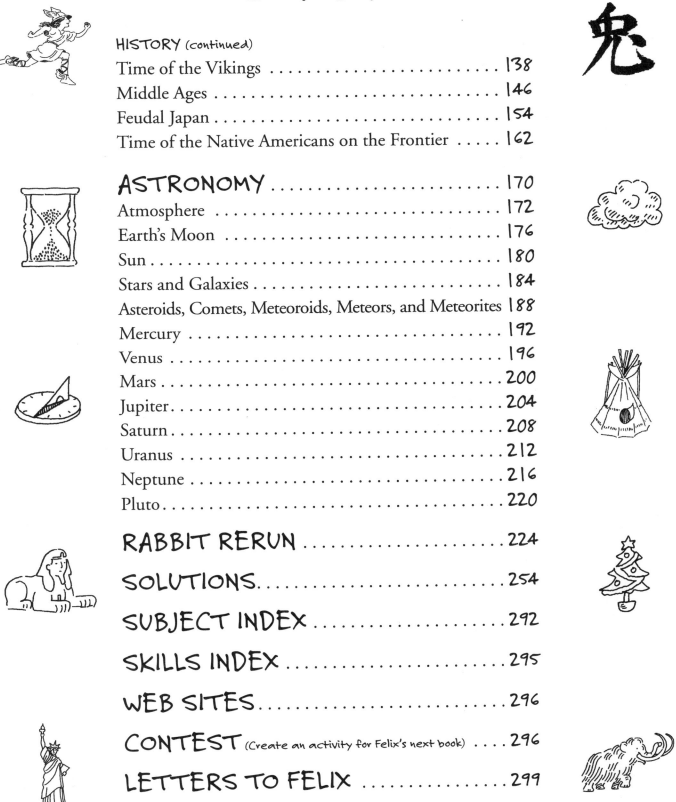

Introduction

Felix the rabbit and his friend Sophie want to share their adventures with you!

You are about to receive letters about all sorts of wonderful things. Write your name on the line after "Dear" at the beginning of each letter. Then you will find out where Felix is and what he's learned.

Felix wrote some of this book, but YOU will finish it! You get to do all the activities that he created. This means that you will be an author and an illustrator!

Tips:
- You do not need to go through this book in order. Find what interests you.
- If something is hard, skip it and come back to it later.
- If you come across a word or place you do not know, circle it and ask an adult about it. You can also look it up in a dictionary, in other books, on a map, or on the Internet.
- Use a pencil in case you change your mind and need to erase.
- Never be afraid to guess!

Here's an important note about history: Before the year 0, years counted down. The letters "B.C.E." after a year mean "Before the Common Era," or before the year 0. For example, the year after 10 B.C.E. was 9 B.C.E. After the year 0, years count up. The letters "C.E." after a year mean "Common Era," or after the year 0. For example, the year after 1999 is 2000.

Felix and Sophie are very happy that they'll be seeing you throughout your journey, and they wish you good luck.

Are you ready? You've got mail . . .

Note to Parents and Teachers

Why this activity book?

FELIX EXPLORES OUR WORLD is distinct among the glut of activity books available today.

Features that set this apart from other activity books (or online sources, for that matter):
- Every activity is marked uncomplicated★, challenging★★, or very challenging★★★. These stars are guides only, and they are used instead of assigning an age range to the book.
- Whimsical letters from Felix and meticulously researched fact pages open each section.
- Important words appear in **bold** and are clearly defined.
- A subject index and a skills index help you help your children address weak spots or focus on specific skills.
- Personality!

Why Felix?

For a rabbit, Felix is incredibly resourceful. He walks upright. He writes letters. He tells time. He's taken a whirlwind tour around the world and into outer space. He's even traveled back in time. This book incorporates all of Felix's adventures. He's a great guide to all that's exciting.

Why for your kids?

Uniquely, this book is never "finished." Even if all the activities are eventually completed, FELIX EXPLORES OUR WORLD remains a personalized album that your child will enjoy reading time and again. It may sound like a stretch for an activity book, but if a rabbit can cross the globe, rocket to the edge of the solar system, and be home in time for dinner, then anything is possible.

Make sure your kids enter the contest on the last page!

Note: Population figures, statistics, and dates are current as of this printing. Most celestial measurements are approximate.

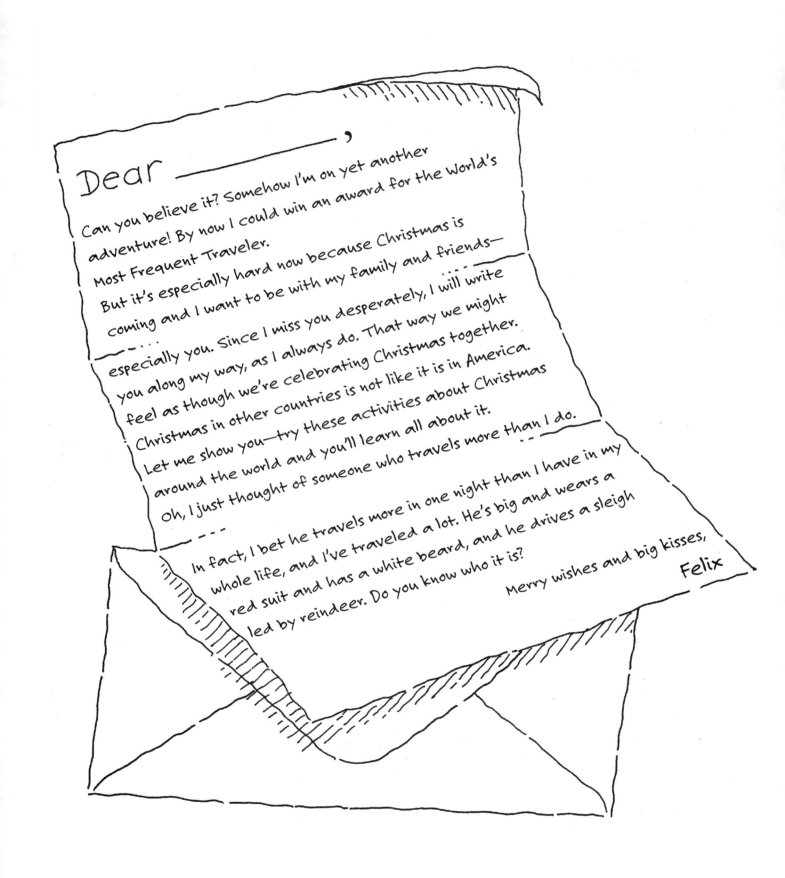

Dear _____,

Can you believe it? Somehow I'm on yet another adventure! By now I could win an award for the World's Most Frequent Traveler.

But it's especially hard now because Christmas is coming and I want to be with my family and friends— especially you. Since I miss you desperately, I will write you along my way, as I always do. That way we might feel as though we're celebrating Christmas together.

Christmas in other countries is not like it is in America. Let me show you—try these activities about Christmas around the world and you'll learn all about it.

Oh, I just thought of someone who travels more than I do. In fact, I bet he travels more in one night than I have in my whole life, and I've traveled a lot. He's big and wears a red suit and has a white beard, and he drives a sleigh led by reindeer. Do you know who it is?

Merry wishes and big kisses,

Felix

CHRISTMAS FACTS

Here are some Christmas-time holidays from around the world. Each country's celebration listed is not necessarily its version of Christmas, but often a holiday observed *in addition* to Christmas. For languages that don't use the English alphabet, the greetings listed are written the way they are spoken in English.

England:
- *Celebration* — Boxing Day
- *Date* — December 26
- *Greeting* — Happy Christmas

Sweden:
- *Celebration* — St. Lucia's Day
- *Date* — December 13
- *Greeting* — God Jul

The Netherlands:
- *Celebration* — Sinterklaas Day, or St. Nicholas Day
- *Date* — December 6
- *Greeting* — Gelukkig Kerstfeest

Germany:
- *Celebration* — Christmas
- *Date* — December 24
- *Greeting* — Fröhliche Weihnachten

Italy:
- *Celebration* — Twelfth Day (Epiphany)
- *Date* — January 6
- *Greeting* — Buon Natale

Russia:
- *Celebration* — Christmas
- *Date* — begins January 6
- *Greeting* — Hristos Razdajetsja

China:
- *Celebration* — Chinese New Year
- *Date* — end of January or beginning of February
- *Greeting* — Sheng Tan Kuai Loh (Mandarin), Gong Tsok Sing Dan (Cantonese)

Australia:
- *Celebration* — Christmas
- *Date* — December 25
- *Greeting* — Merry Christmas

Mexico:
- *Celebration* — Las Posadas (nine total)
- *Dates* — December 16 - 24
- *Greeting* — Feliz Navidad

United States:
- *Celebration* — Christmas
- *Date* — December 25
- *Greeting* — Merry Christmas

No Gloves Required: Christmas in England

In England, the day after Christmas is called Boxing Day. It has nothing to do with the sport. Traditionally, English servants each brought a box to work on December 26. Their employers would put money in it, and that was their holiday present. Today, people still give gifts to those who have helped them during the year, such as the people who deliver newspapers or mail.

Giving to others is one of the most special things you can do, and you don't have to wait until Christmas to do it. You do not have to give something you can hold, like money. It can be your time (like helping your family clean the house or helping your friend with homework), a phone call, advice, a smile, or a hug.

In the boxes, write what you could give to someone else, one gift per month. You can give to a different person each month, the same person every month, or any other way you like. Then check off each gift after you've given it. There are no right or wrong answers.

MONTH	WHAT IS THE GIFT?	FOR WHOM IS THE GIFT?	✔
January			
February			
March			
April			
May			
June			
July			
August			
September			
October			
November			
December			

Swedish and Light: Christmas in Sweden

In Sweden, Christmas begins on St. Lucia's Day, a celebration of a strong woman who lived a long time ago and brought light to the cold Swedish winter. She is St. Lucia, and her name actually means "light." Some believe she glowed and had a halo.

Now, on every December 13, the oldest girl in the family dresses like St. Lucia. She wears a white dress, a red sash, and a crown of evergreen leaves that holds seven candles. Then, along with her sisters (if she has any), she brings coffee and special cakes to her parents. As they walk they sing an old Italian song called "Santa Lucia."

The Swedish use a white dress and candles to look like light and brighten someone's day. Circle any item you could add to your own St. Lucia costume to make more light.

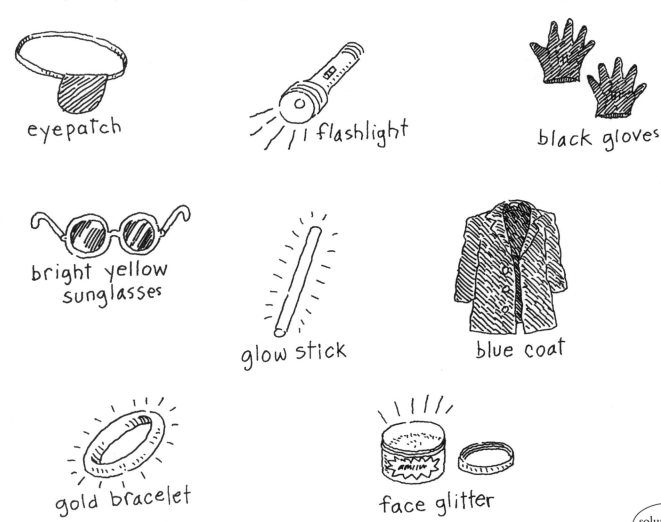

eyepatch

flashlight

black gloves

bright yellow sunglasses

glow stick

blue coat

gold bracelet

face glitter

solution on page 254

13

And the Horse He Rides In On: Christmas in the Netherlands

Christmas is observed quietly in the Netherlands. Often the more festive occasion is Sinterklaas Day, on December 6. Good children anticipate a visit from Sinterklaas (or St. Nicholas), who goes down chimneys and leaves gifts in their wooden shoes, which are left by the fireplace. Like America's Santa Claus, Sinterklaas wears a red robe, but unlike Santa, he rides into town from Spain on his white horse, on December 5. His helper Swarte Piet (Black Pete) accompanies him.

You wake up to discover you've had a visitor in the night. Read the clues and decide if it was Sinterklaas or Santa Claus. Circle the correct name.

1. There are hoof prints from a single animal in your yard.
   Sinterklaas or Santa Claus?

2. There are hoof prints from more than one animal in your yard.
   Sinterklaas or Santa Claus?

3. It is December 6.
   Sinterklaas or Santa Claus?

4. You can't put your shoes on without dumping a few presents out of them first.
   Sinterklaas or Santa Claus?

5. Someone with the initials "SP" signed your parents' guest book.
   Sinterklaas or Santa Claus?

6. You were very good this year.
   Sinterklaas or Santa Claus?

BONUS:
Sinterklaas is a **patron saint**, or a special guardian of a particular group. Guess who he protects.

solution on page 254

Tree History: Christmas in Germany

An old German tale reveals one possible origin of the Christmas tree. An **origin** is the beginning of something.

Martin Luther (1483–1546) was a very important priest who helped form the Protestant church. One peaceful Christmas Eve he went walking through the forest. Snow covered the evergreens and stars twinkled brightly. Luther found the scene so beautiful that he cut down a small fir tree and brought it home. He placed candles in its branches to remind him of the stars from that enchanting night.

These are six trees from the German forest. Three are exactly the same, another two are identical to one another, and one has no match. Write "3" in the three trees that are exactly alike, "2" in the twin trees, and "1" in the unique tree.

Which one do you think Martin Luther would have cut down?_____

solution on page 254

Witch Holiday Is This Again? Christmas in Italy

What holiday reminds you of witches? Halloween? In Italy, a kindly old witch named La Befana is associated with Christmas.

The legends say that La Befana was sweeping when three wise men asked her to visit the Baby Jesus. She said she was too busy, and by the time she changed her mind, she could not find the wise men or the baby. Today she is still searching, which is why she visits each household on Twelfth Night (January 5) and leaves presents for children.

Some of the items below are connected to American holidays. On the line next to each item, write either which holiday it belongs to or write no holiday if it doesn't belong to any.

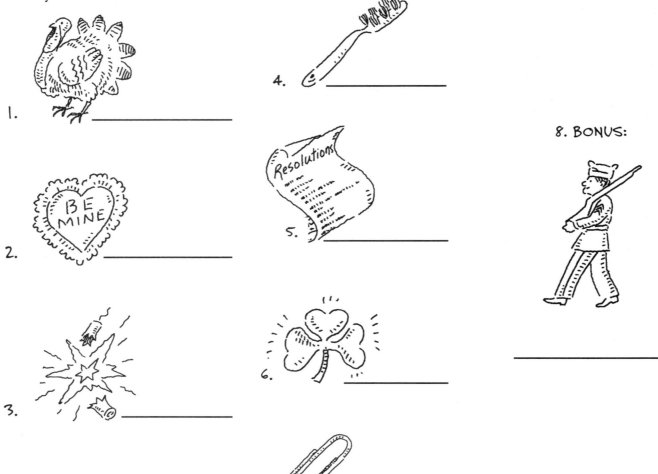

8. BONUS:

solution on page 255

Coldest Cold: Christmas in Russia

The Russian version of Santa Claus has had different names. One is Great Frosty, and another is Grandfather Frost. The temperature is usually below freezing in Russia at Christmas, which is why Grandfather Frost wears a long beard.

What does he look like under that beard? Draw Grandfather Frost after a shave.

★★

Who Came Before: Christmas in China

Christmas is becoming more and more popular in China. Dun Che Lao Ren is the Chinese name for Santa Claus. It means "Christmas Old Man." The Chinese decorate their Christmas trees, called Trees of Light, with paper lanterns and paper flowers.

The Chinese New Year comes in late January or early February. Many feel that it is as joyous as Christmas is in America. It is a special time to honor ancestors, so people hang pictures of family members in the main rooms of their houses. An **ancestor** is a relative who lived long before you. Do you know anything about your ancestors? Do you know what your grandmother's grandmother was like, or where she lived, or what she did?

Pretend it is the Chinese New Year and in celebration, you are able to interview your grandmother's grandmother. She would have lived almost two hundred years ago. You only have time for five questions. What would they be? There are no right or wrong answers.

1. _____
2. _____
3. _____
4. _____
5. _____

What five things about you do you think she would most like to know?

1. _____
2. _____
3. _____
4. _____
5. _____

Down Under the Tree: Christmas in Australia

Australia is very far from America. When it is winter in America, it is summer in Australia. This means Christmas in Australia is usually very hot—sometimes 100°F (38°C). Australians often celebrate on the beach! The weather where Jesus Christ was born was probably warm as well, although today many think of snow when they think of Christmas.

This is a picture of an Australian family's yard. Circle any winter objects you find for Sophie, who will get a lot more use out of them in snowy Ohio than someone would in sunny Australia.

solution on page 255

A Smashing Time: Christmas in Mexico

Once a year at Christmas, Mexican parents allow their children to break something.

This happens during any of nine posada celebrations, in which people get together to reenact Mary and Joseph's difficult journey from Nazareth to Bethlehem in search of shelter. **Posada** is a Spanish word that means shelter or lodging.

What do they break? It's called a **piñata**, and it's a colorfully decorated, hollow figure made out of paper or clay. It is often in the form of an animal or a star. It is stuffed with candy, nuts, fruit, and toys and is hung from the ceiling. The children are blindfolded and take turns trying to hit the piñata with a stick. Once it breaks, the treats fall to the ground for all the children to share.

Take a quick look at the goodies falling from this broken piñata. Without counting, how many pieces do you think there are? _____ Also, draw in your favorite treats.

Mexicans say "Feliz Navidad" to wish you a merry Christmas, but Felix prefers to say

Felix Navidad

solution on page 255

20

Comes But Once a Year: Christmas in the United States

Singing carols is a religious tradition that dates back to medieval England. Today it is still one of the most special Christmas activities because it helps express joy about past miracles and spread good will in the present.

On Christmas Eve, Sophie and Felix will go caroling on their street from 6 P.M. to 7 P.M. Help them plan their route by reading each family's schedule, and then numbering the four houses in the order they should visit so that they don't miss anybody.

HOUSE 1: Sophie's family's house
HOUSE 2: home only until 6:15 P.M.
HOUSE 3: home only from 6:30 to 6:45 P.M.
HOUSE 4: home only from 6:10 to 6:30 P.M.
HOUSE 5: home at 6:50 P.M.

solution on page 255

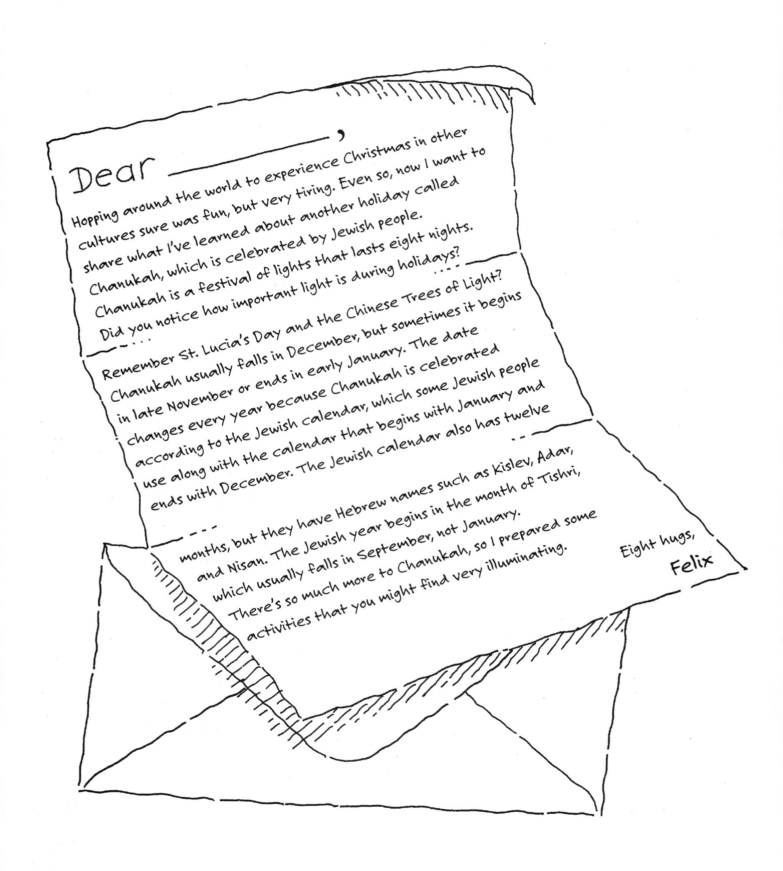

Dear _____,

Hopping around the world to experience Christmas in other cultures sure was fun, but very tiring. Even so, now I want to share what I've learned about another holiday called Chanukah, which is celebrated by Jewish people. Chanukah is a festival of lights that lasts eight nights. Did you notice how important light is during holidays?

Remember St. Lucia's Day and the Chinese Trees of Light? Chanukah usually falls in December, but sometimes it begins in late November or ends in early January. The date changes every year because Chanukah is celebrated according to the Jewish calendar, which some Jewish people use along with the calendar that begins with January and ends with December. The Jewish calendar also has twelve months, but they have Hebrew names such as Kislev, Adar, and Nisan. The Jewish year begins in the month of Tishri, which usually falls in September, not January. There's so much more to Chanukah, so I prepared some activities that you might find very illuminating.

Eight hugs,
Felix

CHANUKAH FACTS

"Chanukah" means:	dedication
Language of the word "Chanukah":	Hebrew
Alternative spellings:	Hanukkah, Hanukah
Start date:	the 25th day of the Hebrew month Kislev (which often falls in December)
Number of days Chanukah lasts:	8
Greeting:	Happy Chanukah

Associated people:

- Judah the Maccabee (?–160 B.C.E.)—leader of the Jewish army
- Antiochus (242–187 B.C.E.)—wicked Greek who was king of Syria
- Mattathias—Judah's elderly father
- John, Simeon, Eleazar, and Jonathon—Judah's brothers and fellow warriors

Symbols:

- menorah—candleholder with nine branches
- shamash—candle used to light the menorah's other candles; means "servant light"
- dreidel—top with a Hebrew letter on each of its four sides
- gelt—money or chocolate coins often given at Chanukah
- latke—potato pancake

★★★

Victory of the Few over the Many

In 165 B.C.E., King Antiochus Epiphanes insisted that Jews pray to the Greek gods rather than to the one God they worshiped. When the Jews refused, the Syrians took over the Temple in Jerusalem and a two-year war began. This was the world's first battle for religious freedom.

Mattathias, his five sons, and many others retreated to the wilderness outside Jerusalem to make a plan. The Syrian army was much bigger than the Jewish one, but under the leadership of Judah the Maccabee, Mattathias's youngest son, they drove the Syrian soldiers from the city. Judah was called "The Hammer" because of his strength.

The Jews were considered the underdogs, but they won. An **underdog** is a person or group that is not expected to succeed, usually because of smallness or inexperience.

Read each competition and circle which of the two you feel is the underdog.

1. **War** — an army with 5,000 soldiers **or** an army with 50,000 soldiers

2. **Nature** — a cat **or** a mouse

3. **Spelling bee** — a student who studied a word list for two hours **or** a student who studied a word list for ten minutes

4. **Football** — a team of eleven players **or** a team of eight players

5. **Art show** — an artist whose paintings are displayed at the front of the gallery **or** an artist whose paintings are displayed in the back of the gallery

BONUS:

6. **Football** — a team of eleven inexperienced players **or** a team of eight experienced players

solution on page 256

A Bright Future

Once the Syrians were gone, the Jews returned to their Temple and immediately began to make it a holy Jewish place again.

To dedicate the Temple they needed special, sacred oil to light the menorah, but they had only enough to last one night. Amazingly, the menorah burned for eight nights. Some say the flame got brighter each night. Meanwhile, the Jews had time to prepare more oil. This is one explanation why Chanukah is celebrated for eight nights.

This activity will also last eight nights. Only the shamash candle is lit on this menorah. Draw in one candle and its flame every night for the next eight nights until it is filled. Each time you do, think of something wonderful that has happened to you. Make each flame brighter than the last. By the way, candles are placed in the menorah from right to left and lit from left to right.

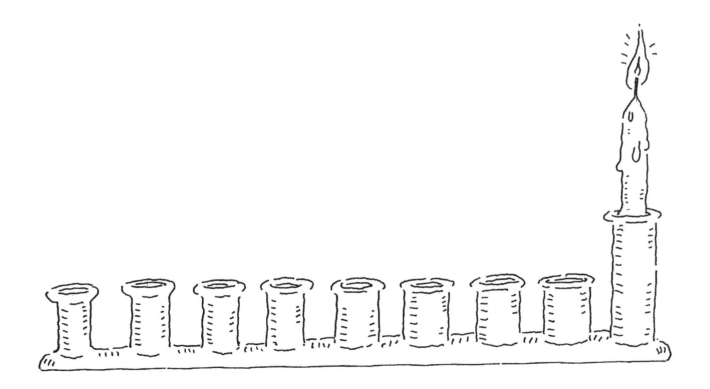

★★★

Spin Control

A popular Chanukah game is spinning a four-sided top called a dreidel.

Each side has a Hebrew letter on it, and they are called nun, gimel, hei, and shin. These letters mean "A great miracle happened there," except in Israel, where the shin is changed to another letter so the sentence means "A miracle happened here."

nun   gimel   hei   shin

How do you play? Everyone starts with a certain number of items and puts one item in the center. Let's use pennies. The first player spins the dreidel, and whichever letter is facing up when it stops determines what action to take.

If it is a **nun**, the spinner **does nothing**. The next player spins.
If it is the **gimel**, the spinner **takes all the pennies** from the center.
If it is the **hei**, the spinner **takes half the pennies** from the center.
If it is the **shin**, the spinner **puts one penny** in the center.

Answer these dreidel questions with the correct number.

1. Sophie plays dreidel with two friends. Each starts with ten pennies and puts one in the center. Sophie spins first, gets the **shin**, and takes the appropriate action. How many pennies are in the center now?
2. By the time Sophie spins next, there are five pennies in the center. She gets the **shin** again! She takes the appropriate action. How many pennies does she have now?
3. Later, on Sophie's last spin, there are ten pennies in the center, and she gets the **hei**. How many pennies does she take from the center?

BONUS:
4. Sophie's friend once played dreidel and got the **nun** every time. How many pennies did he have at the end if he started with twenty? _____

solution on page 256

★★

All I Need Is a Miracle

On Chanukah, Jews remember the miracle of the oil that lasted eight nights. A miracle is an amazing event that may have been caused by a higher power. Do you think miracles still happen today? Can you name any?

Read each event and decide if it is a miracle. Circle yes or no.

1. a baby being born
   yes or no

4. passing a test in school
   yes or no

2. a baseball player hitting a home run
   yes or no

5. doing something bad and not getting caught
   yes or no

3. the creation of the Earth's oceans
   yes or no

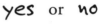

6. working hard to earn enough money for a new toy or game
   yes or no

solution on page 256

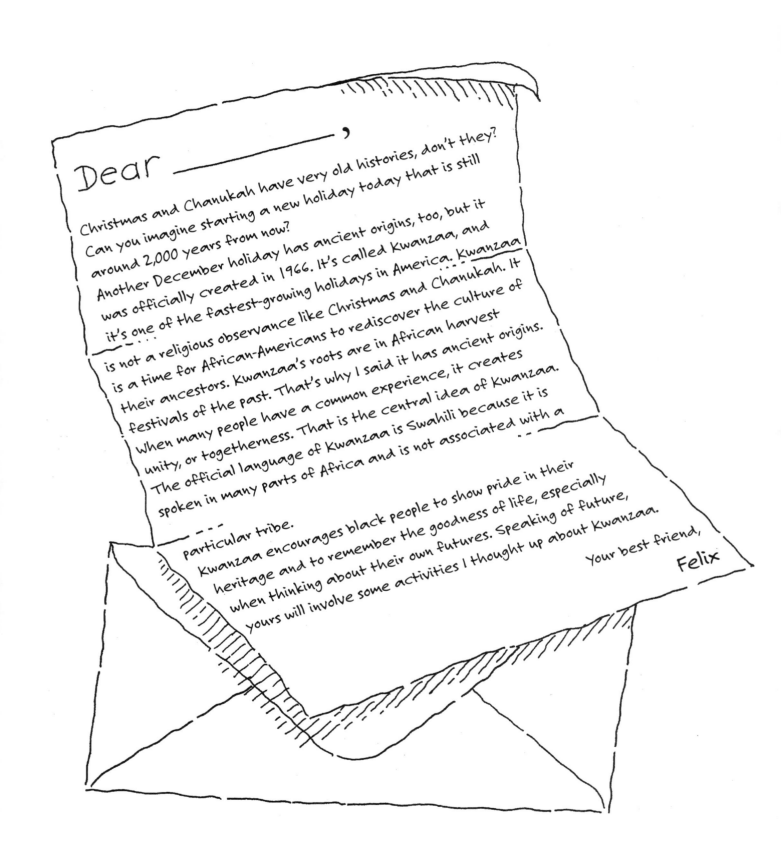

Dear ————,

Christmas and Chanukah have very old histories, don't they? Can you imagine starting a new holiday today that is still around 2,000 years from now?

Another December holiday has ancient origins, too, but it was officially created in 1966. It's called Kwanzaa, and it's one of the fastest-growing holidays in America. Kwanzaa is not a religious observance like Christmas and Chanukah. It is a time for African-Americans to rediscover the culture of their ancestors. Kwanzaa's roots are in African harvest festivals of the past. That's why I said it has ancient origins. When many people have a common experience, it creates unity, or togetherness. That is the central idea of Kwanzaa. The official language of Kwanzaa is Swahili because it is spoken in many parts of Africa and is not associated with a particular tribe.

Kwanzaa encourages black people to show pride in their heritage and to remember the goodness of life, especially when thinking about their own futures. Speaking of future, yours will involve some activities I thought up about Kwanzaa.

Your best friend,

Felix

KWANZAA FACTS

"Kwanzaa" means: first fruits of the harvest

Language of the word "Kwanzaa":   Swahili (an African language)

Alternative spelling: Kwanza

Start date: December 26

Number of days Kwanzaa lasts: 7

Greeting: Habari Gani ("What is the news?" in Swahili)

Associated people:
- Dr. Maulana Ron Karenga (born 1941)—professor who founded the modern Kwanzaa celebration in 1966
- Maya Angelou (born 1928)—author who wrote "The Black Family Pledge," a unifying poem often recited during the Karamu

Symbols:
- mkeka—straw mat on which the kinara and a muhindi for each child or expected child in the family are placed
- kinara—candleholder with seven branches for black, red, and green candles
- mshumaa—the kinara candles, each representing one of seven principles
- muhindi—ear of corn representing children
- Karamu—main feast, held on December 31

★★★

A Candle a Day

During Kwanzaa, when people ask "Habari gani?," you respond with the principle of the day. There are Seven Principles, one for each day of Kwanzaa.

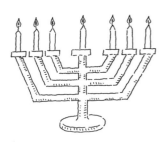

DAY	PRINCIPLE	PRINCIPLE IN SWAHILI
1	unity	Umoja
2	self-determination	Kujichagulia
3	work	Ujima
4	economics	Ujamaa
5	purpose	Nia
6	creativity	Kuumba
7	faith	Imani

One candle is lit each night of Kwanzaa, and then the family discusses the principle of the day. Do you want to practice?

The Seven Principles are repeated below. Draw a line between the principle and the matching example. One is done already.

unity   painting a mural on a wall at school

self-determination   setting a goal to help someone in need

work   believing in your teachers

economics   coming together with family

purpose   helping a neighbor clean his or her garage

creativity   being determined to improve one of your skills

faith   saving money to open a store with a friend some day

solution on page 257

★

In Search of Principles

All of the Seven Principles of Kwanzaa are hidden somewhere in this grid, either across or down. Each word appears only once, in Swahili. Find and circle them.

```
K A J U N I A O T A E
U U K B Z I E Y L V M
U M L B E O P Y A N C
M T A M U W U J I M A
B O L S M C U M O V R
A L E I O M D A E P G
H I Y R J S U L E A S
O U J M A D J F G I O
T V E O N A A I B M I
L A C R E O M P S A K
I B G O L I A O E N M
K U J I C H A G L I A
```

Now see if you can find the principles in your life.

solution on page 257

Original Colors

On Kwanzaa, you might see the flag of African strength. Sometimes it is called the Pan-African flag. It has three horizontal stripes that are the same size. The top stripe is red, the middle is black, and the bottom is green. They are the oldest national colors known to humans, and each has a meaning:

• Red symbolizes the blood of ancestors
• Black symbolizes the black people
• Green symbolizes the land and new life

What are some other things these colors could symbolize? There are no right or wrong answers.

Red _____

Black _____

Green _____

Draw the Pan-African flag. Then next to it, draw another flag that symbolizes the strength of your own family. Next to it, write what each color in your flag means.

solution on page 257

★★

Building a Holiday

In 1966, a professor at a California university named Dr. Maulana Ron Karenga founded Kwanzaa because he noticed there were no American holidays to celebrate the lives and history of African culture. To **found** something means to create something and make it official. Holidays, organizations, and businesses are a few things that can be founded.

It is not easy to create a holiday, but let's try. First, think of something that you want to celebrate, but something that doesn't already have a holiday. What are some examples?

Dr. Karenga

- hardworking students
- pets
- supermarket employees
- astronauts

Pick anything you want to celebrate. Then complete this chart to build your own holiday.

		YOUR HOLIDAY
What is the holiday called?	Kwanzaa	
What does the holiday celebrate?	African culture	
What is the main ceremony?	lighting candles in the kinara every night	
Is there a holiday dinner?	yes, the Karamu on December 31	
Is there a holiday greeting?	yes, "Habari gani?"	
Do you give gifts on the holiday?	yes	
Is there school on the holiday?	yes	

The only thing left to do is to start celebrating!

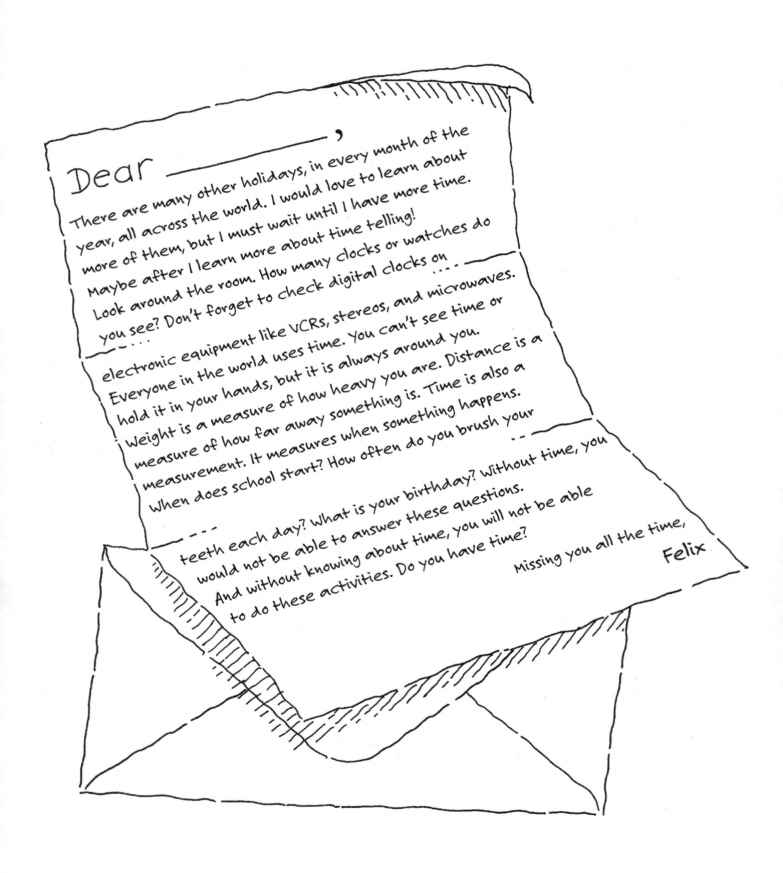

Dear _____,

There are many other holidays, in every month of the year, all across the world. I would love to learn about more of them, but I must wait until I have more time. Maybe after I learn more about time telling!

Look around the room. How many clocks or watches do you see? Don't forget to check digital clocks on electronic equipment like VCRs, stereos, and microwaves.

Everyone in the world uses time. You can't see time or hold it in your hands, but it is always around you. Distance is a measure of how far away something is. Time is also a measure of how heavy you are. Distance is a measurement. It measures when something happens. When does school start? How often do you brush your teeth each day? What is your birthday? Without time, you would not be able to answer these questions. And without knowing about time, you will not be able to do these activities. Do you have time?

Missing you all the time,

Felix

TIME FACTS

Number of seconds in a minute: 60

Number of minutes in an hour: 60

Number of hours in a day: 24

Number of days in a week: 7

Number of days in a month: 30 or 31, except for February, which has either 28 or 29

Number of weeks in a month: 4 or 5

Number of days in a year: 365 (or 366, in a leap year)

Number of weeks in a year: 52

Number of months in a year: 12

Number of years in a century: 100

Number of years in a millennium: 1,000

"A.M." means: before noon (12 o'clock)

"P.M." means: after noon (12 o'clock)

Noon: 12 P.M.

Midnight: 12 A.M.

Roman numerals: I=1, II=2, III=3, IV=4, V=5, VI=6, VII=7, VIII=8, IX=9, X=10, XI=11, XII=12; NOTE: on clocks, 4 is IIII, not IV

Longest day of the year: June 21

Shortest day of the year: December 21

Number of times the Earth revolves around the sun in one year: 1

★

Time Pieces

When you measure your weight, you use pounds or kilograms. When you measure your height, you use feet and inches or meters and centimeters. When you measure time, you use seconds, minutes, hours, days, weeks, months, and years. These are called units of time. A **unit** is another word for piece or section. A second is a piece of a minute, a minute is a piece of an hour, and so on.

Which unit of time would you use in each of these sentences? Write it on the line.

EXAMPLE:

Humans blink their eyes approximately every six seconds.

1. Eating a bowl of cereal usually takes about ten _____

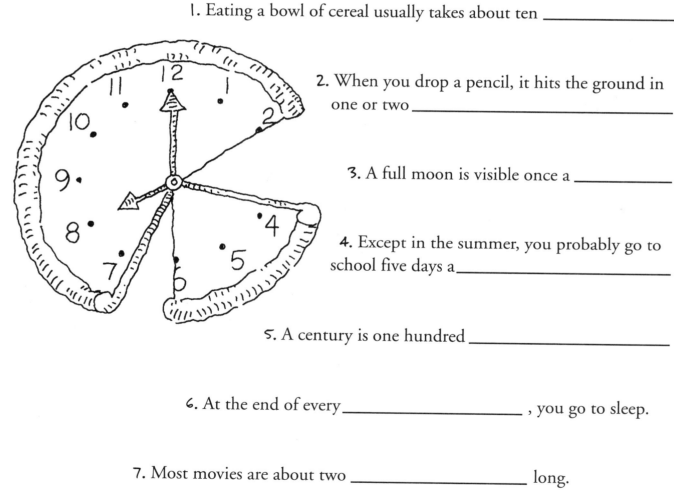

2. When you drop a pencil, it hits the ground in one or two _____

3. A full moon is visible once a _____

4. Except in the summer, you probably go to school five days a_____

5. A century is one hundred _____

6. At the end of every _____ , you go to sleep.

7. Most movies are about two _____ long.

solution on
page 258

38

Help Yourself to Seconds

What do humans and clocks have in common? They both have hands, although their hands look much different.

Clocks have an **hour hand** and a **minute hand**. The hour hand shows what hour it is. The minute hand shows where in the hour it is, and it is longer than the hour hand. Some clocks also have a **second hand**. It shows what second within the minute it is. The second hand moves the fastest, just about as fast as you can count.

It is 8:21 P.M. on the clock below. (By the way, the clock would look the same at 8:21 A.M.) The hour hand is a little past the 8 (Roman numeral VIII) and the minute hand is on the 21st little dot after the 12 (XII). When a clock has a second hand, those little dots or lines are used for both minutes and seconds. For example, in this picture, the second hand is on the 6th little dot after the 12, which is 6 seconds past the minute.

Draw in another second hand for each of the following:

- 1 second past the minute
- half past the minute
- 48 seconds past the minute
- 7 seconds before the next minute

NOTE: The 4 on Roman numeral clocks is written IIII, not IV.

solution on page 258

Save the Day

Did you ever notice how days seem to last longer in the summer? This is because of **daylight saving time**, when people turn their clocks one hour ahead. In America this happens on the first Sunday in April. That way, everyone can enjoy more light in the evening all summer long. On the last Sunday in October, people turn their clocks one hour back for the winter. Then it starts getting dark earlier.

These are two photographs Felix took of Sophie's house in Mansfield, Ohio. One was taken on June 21 and the other on December 21, but they were both taken at the exact same time: 7 P.M. Draw in the colors of the sky in each photograph based on what you know about daylight saving time.

solution on page 258

Let's Do the Time Zone Again

When it is night in America, it is the next day in many faraway places, such as Asia and parts of Europe. The world is too big for everyone to have the same time. That is why there are twenty-four time zones. A **time zone** is an area where all the clocks are set to the same time.

As you go east, you must add an hour every time you cross one of the twenty-four invisible lines that separate time zones. You cross three lines when you fly east from California to New York, so you add three hours to the time. For example, if your watch is still on California time and shows 1 o'clock when you arrive in New York, you must turn it ahead to 4 o'clock. If you call someone back in California when you land in New York at 4 o'clock, it will be 1 o'clock there!

This is a map of the United States (except for Alaska and Hawaii) with three lines that separate four time zones. These are the names of the time zones:

• Eastern
• Central
• Mountain
• Pacific

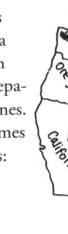

Answer these time zone questions.

1. What time zone is New York City in?_____

2. What time zone is Louisiana in?_____

3. Which time zone includes the fewest states?_____

4. How many states (whole or partial) are in the Mountain time zone?_____

solution on page 258

★★

The Biggest Clock

There was a time when people knew what time it was only if it was sunny. If it was raining or nighttime, they were out of luck.

A **sundial** is a device used to tell time by the sun. The first were used in China more than 4,000 years ago.

You can tell it is 2 o'clock by this sundial because the shadow falls on that line.

Read these situations, and answer these sundial questions.

1. You must be in school at 8 o'clock. What does your sundial look like when you arrive?

2. Your mother leaves the house at 10 A.M. one Saturday for three hours. What time is it when she returns?

3. At 3 o'clock you decide you want to go a store that closes at 5 o'clock and that is one hour away. What is the latest time you can leave to get there by the time it closes?

4. On a camping trip you wake up in the middle of the night to get a drink of water. Your counselor says, "Go to bed. It's 3 o'clock in the morning," but you don't think it's that late. What does your sundial show?

solution on page 259

TIME

Find the Time

Once upon a time, a girl named Meridiem lived in a crowded city with her father and mother. The junkyard they owned was next to their apartment building. Her father called their junkyard "a big pile of things whose time ran out."

Meridiem would wake up with enough time to have a warm breakfast before school. When she had time she would stop at a fruit stand to buy a fresh apple with some of the money her parents gave her for lunch.

"How are you today?" Meridiem asked the fruit-stand vendor.

"Tired from getting up so early," the fruit-stand vendor said. "And still I never have enough time to do what I want."

Meridiem nodded sadly and kept walking. A clock on a building showed the time to be 7:50 A.M. She had time to stop at the newsstand to look at her favorite magazine.

"Good morning," she said to the newsstand vendor.

"There was a time when every morning was good," the newsstand vendor said. "Now people don't have time to read, and I don't sell many papers."

"I'm sorry. I would buy one if I had enough money."

"Don't worry about money, Meridiem. It's time that is important. Spend it wisely."

It was almost 8:00 A.M., and if Meridiem was late for school one more time, she knew she would get in trouble. She rushed.

That night Meridiem thought about the two vendors. She couldn't give them more time, but she could make time nicer for them. She had an idea.

In the morning she got up extra early so she could go to the junkyard. It took her some time before she found two antique clocks that still worked. She cleaned them and found that they looked quite distinguished. Then she left for school.

First she stopped at the fruit vendor's stand and gave him one of the clocks.

"Thank you, Meridiem. I will keep this clock on my stand all day to remind me how much time I really do have."

Meridiem smiled and hurried to the newsstand, where she gave the vendor the other clock.

"What a surprise. Thank you! But I told you to spend your time wisely. Why did you get this wonderful clock for me?"

"I thought it was so handsome that people might stop and ask what time it is, and then they might buy a paper," she said. "Besides, I had a little extra time this morning."

How many times does the word ~~time~~ appear in the story?_____

solution on pages 259–260

43

★

Blackout

Last night a huge storm knocked out the electricity for a few hours in Sophie's neighborhood. Her watch shows that it is 7:30 A.M.

Circle any clock whose time needs to be adjusted.

solution on page 260

Whole Millennium Ahead of You

One hundred years is a century. One thousand years is a millennium, which means that there are ten centuries in one millennium. A new millennium begins in 2001.

What are your personal goals for the new millennium? Write your top five below.

1. _____
2. _____
3. _____
4. _____
5. _____

What are your dreams for the world for the new millennium? Write your top five below.

1. _____
2. _____
3. _____
4. _____
5. _____

★★★

Time Enough at Last

Each of these activities lasts a different amount of time. Number them from 1–5, with 1 being the activity that takes the least amount of time and 5 being the activity that takes the most amount of time.

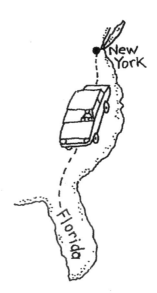

drive a car from
New York to Florida

_____

spell your first name

_____

eat a banana

_____

watch your favorite cartoon

_____

get a good night's sleep

_____

solution on page 260

Father of All Clocks

This is a grandfather clock, or pendulum clock. The **pendulum** is the long rod with a round object at the bottom. It swings back and forth, and helps the clock run properly. It's a nice way to tell time, don't you think?

Does this clock look like a grandfather? Of course not. Although the Dutch scientist Christiaan Huygens (1629–1695) invented the pendulum clock in 1657, it got its famous nickname in 1876 because of a popular American song by Henry Clay Work (1832–1884) called "My Grandfather's Clock."

What would **a grandmother clock** look like? Draw it below. Also draw the following:

- a mother clock
- a father clock
- a sister or brother clock
- a son or daughter clock

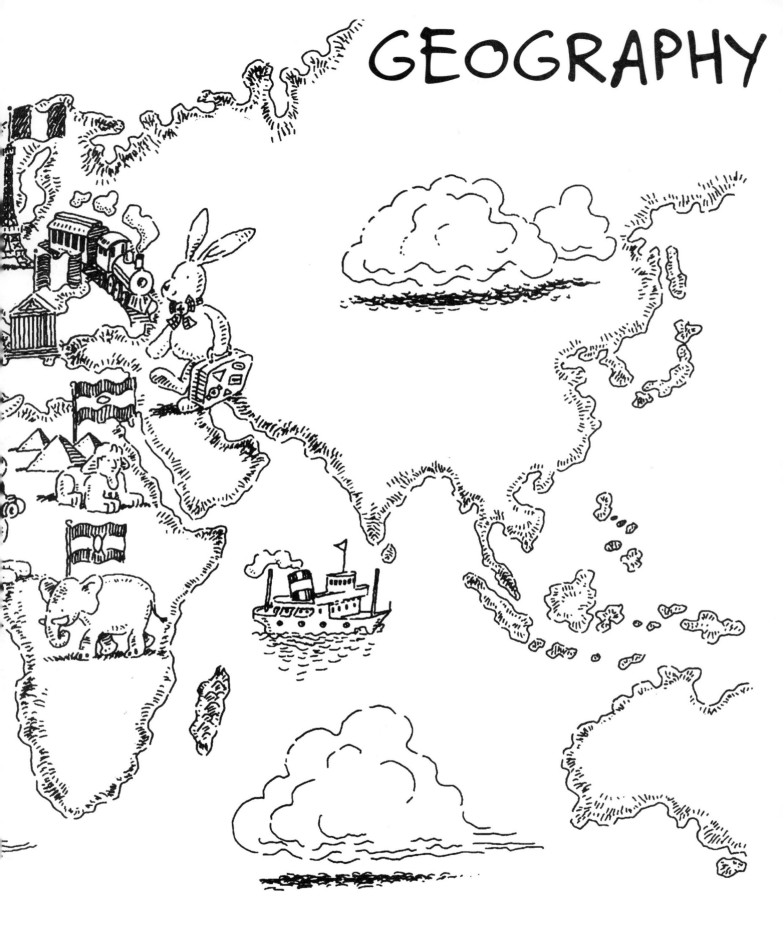

GEOGRAPHY

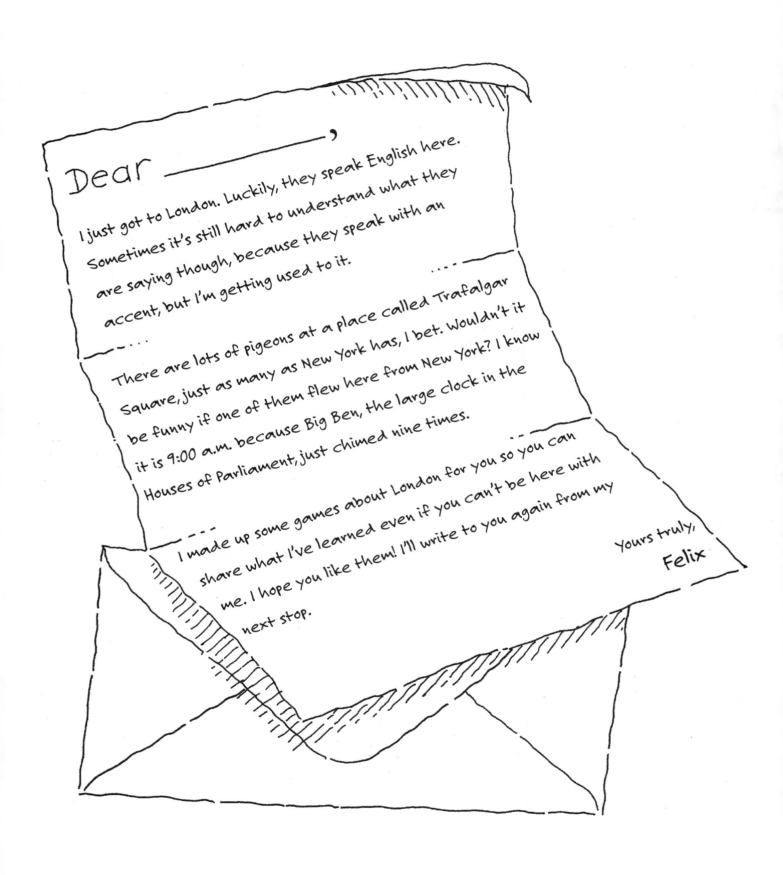

Dear _____,

I just got to London. Luckily, they speak English here. Sometimes it's still hard to understand what they are saying though, because they speak with an accent, but I'm getting used to it.

There are lots of pigeons at a place called Trafalgar Square, just as many as New York has, I bet. Wouldn't it be funny if one of them flew here from New York? I know it is 9:00 a.m. because Big Ben, the large clock in the Houses of Parliament, just chimed nine times.

I made up some games about London for you so you can share what I've learned even if you can't be here with me. I hope you like them! I'll write to you again from my next stop.

Yours truly,
Felix

LONDON FACTS

Country: England

Capital city: London

Official language: English

Continent: Europe

Number of countries in Europe: 48

London's population: 6,770,400

England's climate: rains year-round, sometimes dry and cold

Traditional currency: pound sterling

Some historic British:
- William I (1027–1087), king of England from 1066 to 1087, known as William the Conqueror, who ordered a land survey in 1086
- Sir Winston Churchill (1874–1965), prime minister from 1940 to 1945 and 1951 to 1955
- The Beatles, rock-and-roll band from 1962 to 1970
- Margaret Thatcher (born 1925), prime minister from 1979 to 1990

Some symbols associated with London:
- London Bridge
- Thames River
- Westminster Abbey
- Big Ben
- Houses of Parliament
- Union Jack (official flag of England)
- bobbies
- high tea (drinking tea in the late afternoon)
- royal family
- double decker bus

London

★★

Cartoons in the Car Park

In London, what Americans call a parking lot is known as a **car park**. This cartoon strip shows a conversation in a car park between a man and a British police officer, called a **bobby**. Bobbies are named after Sir Robert Peel, who set up the Metropolitan Police of London in 1828.

A scene in a car park involving a bobby and another man is pictured below. In the word bubbles, write what these characters are saying.

★★

Talk of the Town

This is the front page of the newspaper from the day that Felix arrived in London. Fill in the blank spaces. Write the headline on the dotted line, your **byline** (the author's name), and the main story. Then draw the photograph that goes with your story.

The London Herald

£1   Monday, August 1, 1994   Weather: Rain

- -

Exclusive by _____

_____

_____

_____

_____

_____

_____

Photo by _____

★★★

Ahead of Time

Sophie lives in Mansfield, Ohio. Did you know that when it is noon at Sophie's house in Mansfield, it is 5:00 in the evening in London? London, England, is five hours ahead of Mansfield (and the rest of the eastern United States, too!) because of the different time zones.

Circle or write the answer to each question about time differences between Mansfield and London.

1. Felix hears Big Ben (a gigantic clock in the Houses of Parliament) chime the hour. It is 12:00 in the afternoon. What time is it at Sophie's house in Mansfield?

   A. 5:00 in the evening
   B. 12:00 in the afternoon
   C. 7:00 in the morning

2. Who goes to bed first, Sophie in Mansfield or Felix in London?

   A. Sophie
   B. Felix

3. When it reaches midnight on New Year's Eve in Mansfield, is it already the new year in London?

   A. it is already the new year
   B. it is not yet the new year

4. Why wouldn't Sophie in Mansfield want to call Felix in London right before she goes to sleep, at 8:00 at night?

   _____

5. Sophie's school starts at 9:00 in the morning. If school in London ends at 3:00 in the afternoon, are London children still in school when Sophie starts school?

   A. yes
   B. no

solution on page 261

Baby, the Rain Must Fall

London gets a lot of rain. This is a street scene in London where it suddenly started pouring. No one seems prepared! Help everyone stay dry by drawing in their protection from the rain. (HINT: Draw umbrellas, windshield wipers, awnings . . .)

★★

London Jumble

Unscramble the following words. Each one has something to do with London.

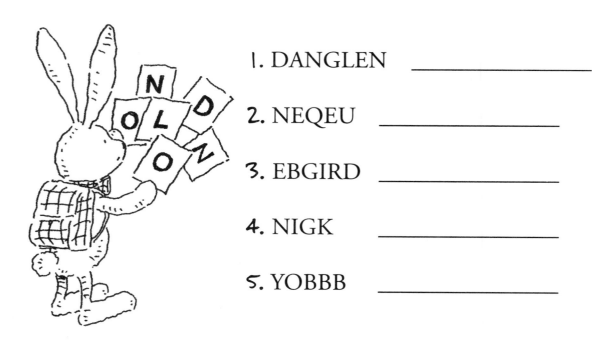

1. DANGLEN   _____

2. NEQEU   _____

3. EBGIRD   _____

4. NIGK   _____

5. YOBBB   _____

BONUSES:

1. STEHAM   _____

   (A river flowing through London.)

2. ONIUN CAJK   _____

   (The nickname for the British flag.)

3. BLUDOE KREDEC   _____

   (A famous kind of British bus.)

solution on page 261

License to Drive

People in the United States drive on the right side of the street. In London, and everywhere in England, people drive on the left side of the street. This is not "backwards." British people have a different road system, just as they have different kinds of money, government, food, and sports.

Here are some license plates that Felix saw on cars either in England or in the United States. Circle the country where you think he spotted each license plate. Think of the customs or characteristics of each location to help you decide.

England or United States?

England or United States?

England or United States?

England or United States?

solution on page 261

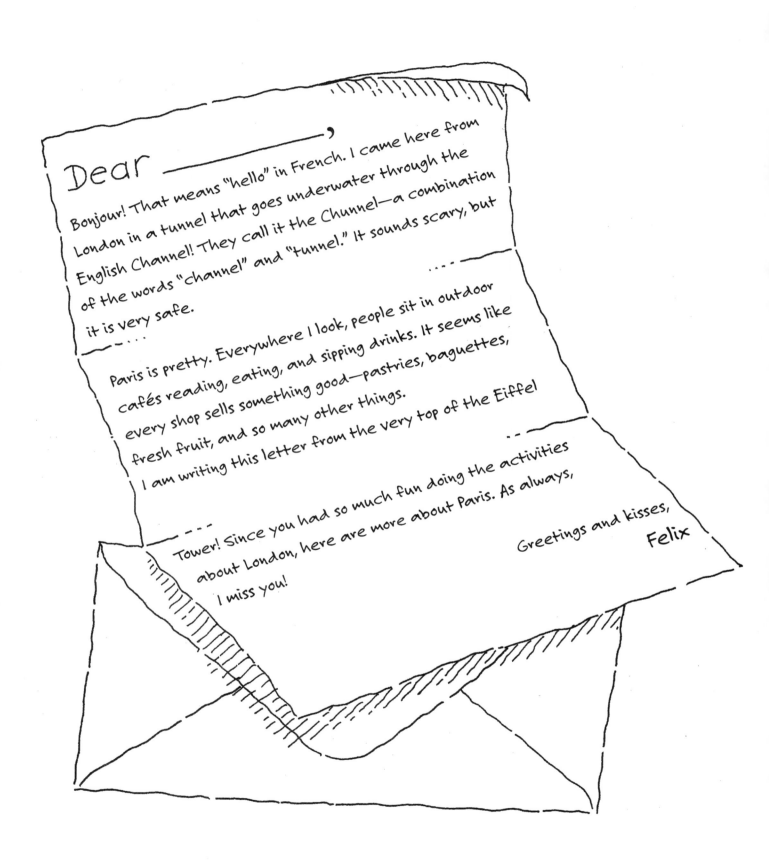

Dear _____,

Bonjour! That means "hello" in French. I came here from London in a tunnel that goes underwater through the English Channel! They call it the Chunnel—a combination of the words "channel" and "tunnel." It sounds scary, but it is very safe.

Paris is pretty. Everywhere I look, people sit in outdoor cafés reading, eating, and sipping drinks. It seems like every shop sells something good—pastries, baguettes, fresh fruit, and so many other things.

I am writing this letter from the very top of the Eiffel Tower! Since you had so much fun doing the activities about London, here are more about Paris. As always, I miss you!

Greetings and kisses,

Felix

PARIS FACTS

Country: France

Capital city: Paris

Official language: French

Continent: Europe

*Number of countries
in Europe:*   48

Paris's population: 2,188,918

France's climate: cold winters and hot, dry summers

Traditional currency: French franc

Some historic French: • Joan of Arc (circa 1412–1431), teenage girl who fought for France
                                  against England in 1430
                                • Napoleon Bonaparte I (1769–1821), emperor of France from
                                  1804 to 1815
                                • Charles de Gaulle (1890–1970), president of France from
                                  1959 to 1969

*Some symbols associated
with Paris:*
                                • Notre-Dame Cathedral
                                • Champs Elysées (street famous for its shops and restaurants)
                                • Arc de Triomphe
                                • Eiffel Tower
                                • Louvre (museum that houses the Mona Lisa)
                                • baguette (long loaf of bread)

• Paris

★★★

One Word Leads to Another

Fill in each box below with a word that begins with the letter at the left and also fits the category at the top. There can be more than one correct answer. Two boxes are already filled in to help you get started.

	COUNTRY	CITY	TYPE OF FOOD	SCHOOL SUBJECT	BODY OF WATER
P	Portugal				
A					
R					
I					
S			spaghetti		

solution on page 262

The View from Here

Felix took the elevator all the way to the top of the Eiffel Tower in Paris. He is looking down at the city, and he sees some things that seem too big. After all, he is 984 feet (300 meters) up, and everything looks much smaller from so high. Color the five objects that are too big.

solution on page 262

★★★

Oddballs

When Felix visits Paris, he is surprised that the people at his hotel and on the street don't notice him. Wouldn't you think that a rabbit with a suitcase would stand out?

In each group of words below, one word does not belong. Find the oddball and circle it. On the line, write what makes it different.

1. Baguette   Cheese
   Salad   Cathedral
   Oddball because: _____

2. Pizza   Baguette
   Croissant   Quiche
   Oddball because: _____

3. Baguette   Wine
   Cheese   Salad
   Oddball because: _____

4. Church   Ball
   Bread   Baguette
   Oddball because: _____

5. Eiffel Tower   Notre-Dame Cathedral
   Champs Elysées   Arc de Triomphe
   Oddball because: _____

6. Dressing   Carrot
   Fries   Toast
   Oddball because: _____

7. Paris   France
   Italy   Canada
   Oddball because: _____

8. Seine River   Loire River
   Rhône River   Nile River
   Oddball because: _____

solution on page 262

★★

Speak French

In the United States, people speak many languages. The one most often spoken today is English. In France, everyone uses French. Below are some familiar objects with their French and English names next to them.

Study the pictures and the foreign names, and then use your new French words to finish the sentences below. Some of the words are written in already to get you started.

1. _____ *entend* _____ .
   The boy   hears   the wind.

2. _____ *achète* _____ .
   The girl   buys   a hat.

3. _____ *porte*   _____ *et*   _____ .
   The boy   wears   gloves   and   a scarf.

4. _____ *déblaye* _____ *avec* _____ .
   The girl   shovels   snow   with   a shovel.

solution on page 263

★★★

Can You Spare a Dollar?

In the United States, the dollar bill is the unit of **currency** (money). In France, the traditional unit is the French franc. "Franc" sounds the way you say the man's name Frank. One dollar equals about five French francs. If a bottle of juice in the United States costs one dollar, you would need five French francs to buy it in France. Below are some questions that compare dollar bills and French francs.

1. If a soda costs $1.00 in the United States, how many French francs would you need to buy it in France? _____

2. If an ice cream cone costs $2.00 in the United States, how many French francs would you need to buy it in France? _____

3. If a paperback book costs $6.00 in the United States, how many French francs would you need to buy it in France? _____

solution on
page 263

What's for Lunch?

Jean-Pierre is having fun at this French bistro. The word **bistro** means a small restaurant in both French and English. Jean-Pierre has just placed his order. Find and color the three hidden foods that he has ordered.

solution on page 263

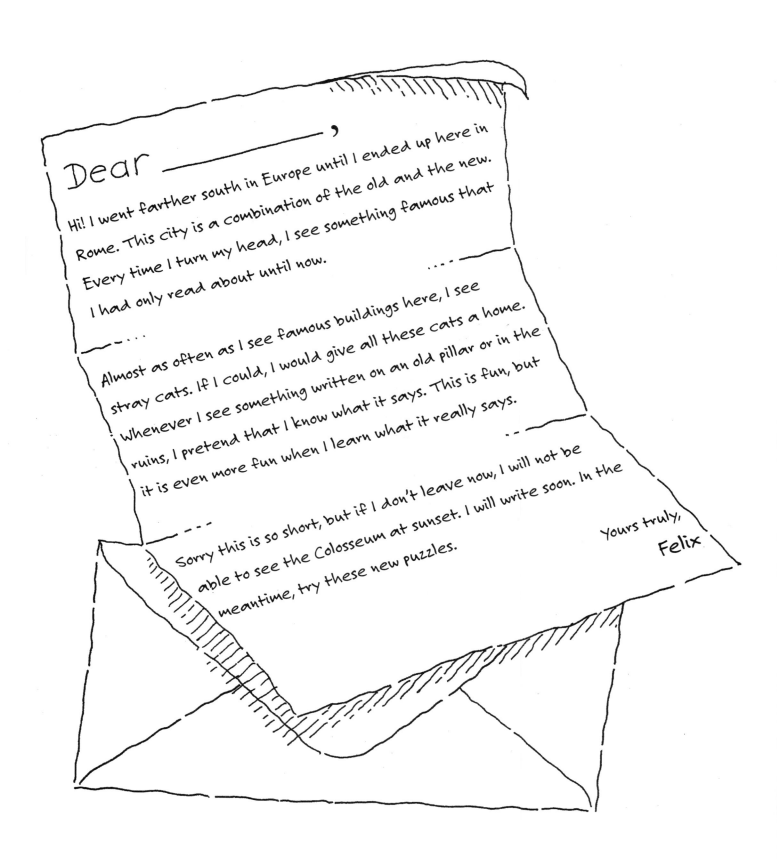

Dear _____,

Hi! I went farther south in Europe until I ended up here in Rome. This city is a combination of the old and the new. Every time I turn my head, I see something famous that I had only read about until now.

Almost as often as I see famous buildings here, I see stray cats. If I could, I would give all these cats a home. Whenever I see something written on an old pillar or in the ruins, I pretend that I know what it says. This is fun, but it is even more fun when I learn what it really says.

Sorry this is so short, but if I don't leave now, I will not be able to see the Colosseum at sunset. I will write soon. In the meantime, try these new puzzles.

Yours truly,
Felix

ROME FACTS

Country:	Italy
Capital city:	Rome
Official language:	Italian
Continent:	Europe
Number of countries in Europe:	48
Rome's population:	2,817,227
Italy's climate:	hot, sunny summers and short, cold winters
Traditional currency:	Italian lira

Some historic Italians:

- Romulus, legendary man who founded Rome in 753 B.C.E.
- Julius Caesar (100–44 B.C.E.), dictator of the Roman world who was assassinated on March 15
- Christopher Columbus (circa 1446–1506), navigator attributed with discovering America in 1492

Some symbols associated with Rome:

- Pantheon
- Vatican
- Sistine Chapel
- Spanish Steps
- Trevi Fountain
- Forum
- Colosseum

★★★

Rome Was Built in a Day

When Felix was looking through his suitcase, he found a few letters he wrote to Sophie from Rome. He never sent them because he realized that each one has an anomaly. An **anomaly** is a mistake or a word that seems out of place. This sentence has an anomaly: "My friend's new bicycle has a horn, red reflectors, and a very nice water fountain." The anomaly is "water fountain." Have you ever seen a bike with a water fountain?

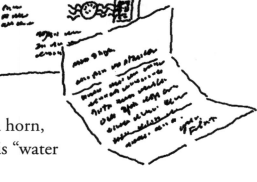

Underline the anomalies in each of these letters that Felix wrote.

1.
> Dear Sophie,
> I just got to Rome. People say that this is the most beautiful city in England, but I really don't know because it's the only one I have visited. I really wish you were here with me. I will be home soon.
>
> Love, Felix

2.
> Dearest Sophie,
> Here I am in Rome. Everyone is so nice, and the food is delicious, especially the ice cream! Because Rome is an island, I had to take a boat to get here. Have you ever been on boat? I will write to you soon.
>
> Yours truly, Felix

3.
> Hi Sophie!
> Traveling has been so much fun! In Europe it is easy to see lots of things because the countries are close together. I am still in Rome because I wanted to practice my French. It must not be very good because people keep giving me funny looks. Don't forget about me!
>
> Best wishes from your Felix

4.
> Dear Sophie,
> Rome is so historic! Did you know that they only have two subway lines here? If they built more, it could be dangerous to the ancient buildings like the Colosseum, because subways could loosen the ground beneath them. The Colosseum is so old that the elevators in it don't work and a big chunk of it is missing. It doesn't look like they are ever going to fix it. Oh, well. I miss you!
>
> Kisses, Felix

The title of this game is also a kind of anomaly! There is a popular saying, "Rome wasn't built in a day." Can you imagine building a whole city in one day?

solution on page 263

★★

Eternally Rome

Felix visited modern Rome, but while he was there, he learned a lot about its history. He invented a secret code for Sophie to share what he learned. Felix assigned a number to every letter of the alphabet. First, translate the code in the boxes below. Next, answer the questions Felix asks Sophie by writing the correct letter in the box above each number.

1 = <u>A</u>	2 = <u>B</u>	3 = __	4 = __	5 = __	6 = __	7 = __	8 = __	9 = __
10 = __	11 = __	12 = __	13 = __	14 = __	15 = __	16 = __	17 = __	18 = __
19 = __	20 = __	21 = __	22 = __	23 = __	24 = __	25 = __	26 = __	

1. Who is the person we think founded Rome?

___ ___ ___ ___ ___ ___ ___
18 15 13 21 12 21 19

4. Which river flows through Rome?

___ ___ ___ ___ ___
20 9 2 5 18

2. What is the white robe called that Romans wore?

___ ___ ___ ___
20 15 7 1

5. What word describes the government of early Rome?

___ ___ ___ ___ ___ ___ ___ ___
18 5 16 21 2 12 9 3

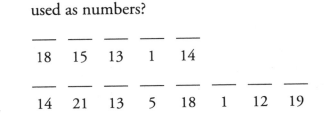

3. What kind of metal did the Romans use to make tools and weapons?

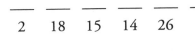

___ ___ ___ ___ ___ ___
2 18 15 14 26 5

6. What is the name for the symbols that Romans used as numbers?

___ ___ ___ ___ ___
18 15 13 1 14

___ ___ ___ ___ ___ ___ ___ ___
14 21 13 5 18 1 12 19

BONUS: Rome is nicknamed the ___ ___ ___ ___ ___ ___ ___   ___ ___ ___ ___
5 20 5 18 14 1 12   3 9 20 25

solution on pages 263–264

★★

Mystery History

Someone sent Sophie a strange letter with boxes that have words written inside them. Sophie has never seen some of the words before. The letter says: "Shade the boxes that contain a word that has something to do with Rome. Then you will know who sent this letter." Sophie is pretty sure she already knows who sent it, but she wants you to help her shade the right boxes anyway. There are eight boxes that have something to do with Rome. After you shade them, look at this page from a little farther away, and you will get a hint as to the identity of the letter-writer.

Colosseum	Spanish Steps	Trevi Fountain
Sistine Chapel	Big Ben	Statue of Liberty
Pantheon	Forum	Sphinx
"Ciao!"	tepees	Eiffel Tower
lira	chopsticks	knights

CLUES:

- The Forum was the meeting place for public discussions in ancient Rome.

- "Ciao!" is the Italian way to say "hello" or "goodbye."

- The Trevi Fountain is a fountain in Rome with a statue of Neptune, the ocean god.

- The Spanish Steps are a long, winding outdoor set of stairs in Rome where people sit in nice weather.

- The Colosseum is the large oval amphitheater in Rome with a piece of its wall missing.

- Lira is the traditional Italian unit of money.

- The Pantheon is an ancient temple in Rome that was built in the shape of a circle with a hole in the roof so that light could come in.

- The Sistine Chapel is the chapel at the Vatican (the palace where the Pope lives). Its ceiling is decorated with a famous painting by the artist Michelangelo.

Who do you think wrote the letter? _____

solution on page 264

Chunk of the Colosseum

The Colosseum is a giant oval amphitheater where the ancient Romans used to watch sports and other contests. It took about ten years to build, from the year 70 to the year 80. Today the Colosseum is damaged, but it is still standing! Because the Colosseum is so old, it is not surprising that a chunk of it is missing.

Only one of the chunks below could be the missing piece of the Colosseum. The others do not fit. Circle the missing piece.

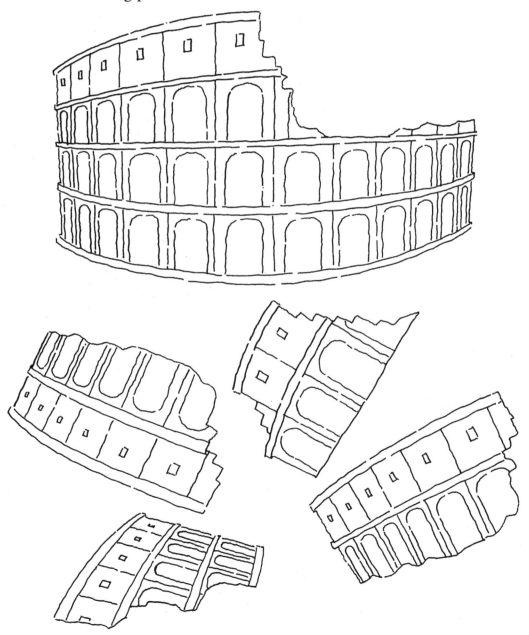

solution on page 264

★★

Youville

Rome is a very old city. Some structures in Rome were built thousands of years ago, but others are very new. These newer buildings had to be constructed around the old ones. Anyone who builds something in Rome has to be very careful not to harm any of its delicate history.

Plan your own city. Below is a list of buildings your city will need. The grid is the blank city map. The lines are the streets. Write the name of each building where you want the building to be placed on the city map, and add any other buildings that you think are important. In your city, everything will be brand new!

bank	fire station	library	place of worship	restaurant
city hall	grocery store	movie theater	police station	school
department store	hospital	pharmacy	post office	your house

What is the name of your city? _____

Coins in the Fountain

Beautiful fountains are a popular attraction in Rome. There is something romantic about fountains, and Rome is a romantic city. People throw coins into fountains for different reasons, but they often do so to make a wish.

Lira is the traditional Italian unit of money, and one lira is worth about $1/17$ of a cent. This means it would take seventeen lire to equal one penny. If a candy bar cost a dollar in the United States, you would need 1,700 lire to buy the same candy bar in Italy!

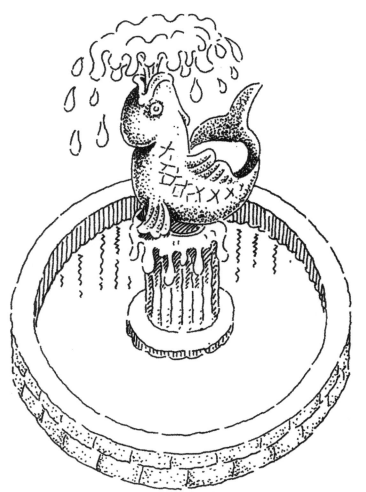

Here are pictures of a 100-lira coin and a nickel. They are worth about the same amount of money.

100-lira   nickel

Draw a picture of each coin in the fountain to the left, and make a wish on each one. Write your wishes on the lines. Hopefully your wishes will come true!

WISH 1: _____

WISH 2: _____

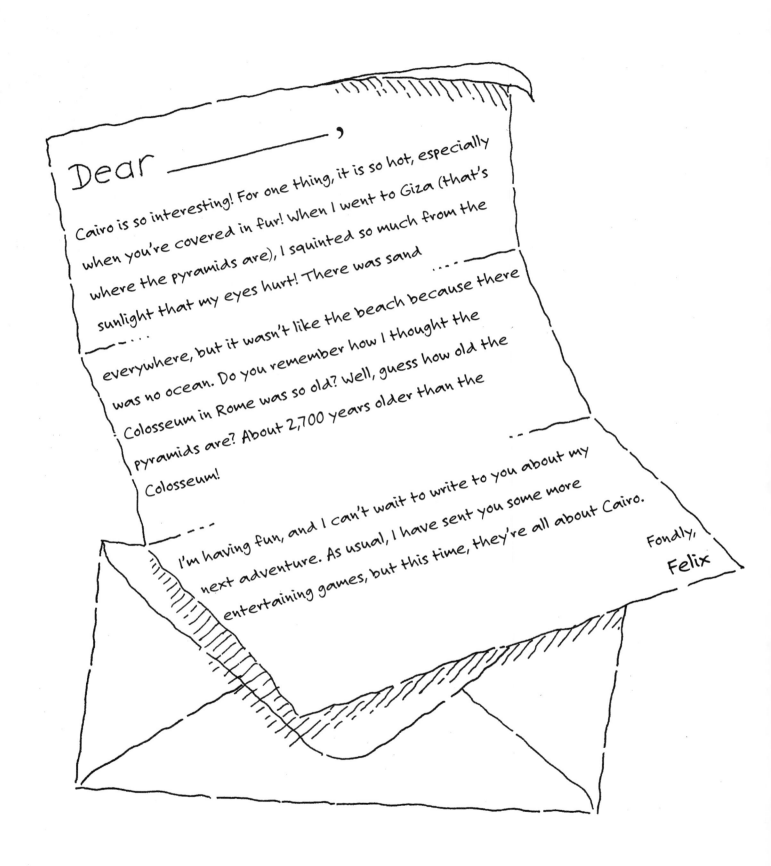

Dear _____,

Cairo is so interesting! For one thing, it is so hot, especially when you're covered in fur! When I went to Giza (that's where the pyramids are), I squinted so much from the sunlight that my eyes hurt! There was sand everywhere, but it wasn't like the beach because there was no ocean. Do you remember how I thought the Colosseum in Rome was so old? Well, guess how old the pyramids are? About 2,700 years older than the Colosseum!

I'm having fun, and I can't wait to write to you about my next adventure. As usual, I have sent you some more entertaining games, but this time, they're all about Cairo.

Fondly,
Felix

CAIRO FACTS

Country:	Egypt
Capital city:	Cairo
Official language:	Arabic
Continent:	Africa
Number of countries in Africa:	52
Cairo's population:	6,325,000
Egypt's climate:	mostly desert, hot
Currency:	Egyptian pound

Cairo●

Some historic Egyptians:
- Ramses II, king of Egypt from 1292 to 1225 B.C.E.
- Cleopatra (69–30 B.C.E.), queen of Egypt from 51 to 49 B.C.E. and from 48 to 30 B.C.E.
- Anwar Sadat (1918–1981), president of Egypt from 1970 to 1981 who worked for peace with Israel

Some symbols associated with Cairo:
- pyramids and the Sphinx (both in Giza, just outside Cairo)
- Sahara Desert (the largest desert in the world)
- pharaohs (ancient kings of Egypt)

★★★

Word from Egypt

Write the correct answers on the opposite page to complete the crossword.

ACROSS

1. Capital of Egypt
3. The Sphinx has the body of a _____
5. Egypt is in the north_____ part of Africa
6. In ancient Greece, the Sphinx was a myth; in the Egyptian desert, it is a _____ stone figure (HINT: If it is the opposite of a myth, it is _____.)
7. Egypt is one of the _____-two countries in Africa
10. In 1978, Egypt was not the last, but rather one of the _____ Arab countries to begin making peace with Israel
11. The Mediterranean is the closest ___ to Cairo
12. Which is not a major product of Egypt: corn or cotton?
13. Suburb of Cairo where the pyramids and the Sphinx are found
14. Of the _____ wonders of the ancient world, the pyramids are the oldest and only ones that still survive

DOWN

2. Official language of Egypt
3. Cairo is near the Sahara, the _____ desert in the world
4. This river runs through Cairo; at 4,160 miles (6,670 kilometers), it is the longest in the world
8. What shape is the face of a pyramid?
9. Another word for an ancient king of Egypt
12. Cairo is the biggest _____ in Africa, based on population

Five squares in the crossword puzzle are shaded. Write the letters from those squares in these boxes in any order.

☐ ☐ ☐ ☐ ☐

Now unscramble those letters to discover the answer to this question: What kind of bird is featured on the Egyptian flag?

☐ ☐ ☐ ☐ ☐

solution on page 265

★★

Puzzle of the Pyramids

It is impressive that the pyramids outside Cairo are still standing. They were built sometime around 2500 B.C.E., a long time before the big construction machines that you see today were invented! How do you think these huge triangle-shaped structures were built? Draw a scene below showing the pyramids being built.

Either Or

Each of these questions or statements about Cairo has two choices for an answer. Circle the correct answer.

1. What kind of climate does Cairo have?

   cold   or   hot

2. What continent is Cairo on?

   Africa   or   Asia

3. Cairo is a country.

   true   or   false

4. What animal might you see in Cairo?

   a camel   or   a penguin

5. Someone who lives in Cairo, Egypt, could be called what?

   an Egyptian   or   an Italian

6. Do you want to visit Cairo?

   yes   or   no

solution on page 265

★

Solid Work

Although they are not actually in the city itself, the great pyramids are associated with Cairo. A pyramid is a three-dimensional triangle. **Three-dimensional** means something is solid, like a book, a bird, a planet, or a glass of water. It does not mean that something has three sides. By the way, you are three-dimensional!

A square is not three-dimensional since it is four lines on a page. A box is three-dimensional. It is a three-dimensional square!

Some of these things are three-dimensional. Some are not. Circle the things that are three-dimensional.

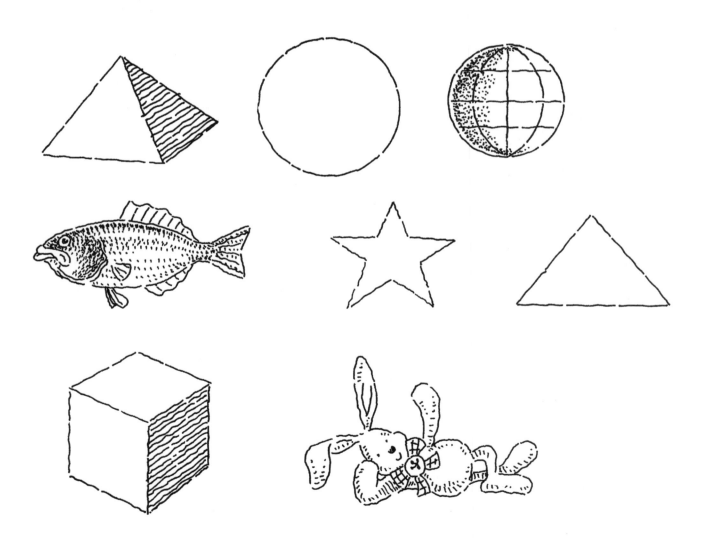

solution on page 265

Paper Chase

You just found a piece of **papyrus**, a thin material made from a special plant. Ancient Egyptians used to write on papyrus. Now is your chance!

Create a treasure map on this piece of papyrus that Sophie could use to find jewelry hidden by old pharaohs of Egypt somewhere in the desert. Make sure to include some obstacles. Don't forget that "X" marks the spot," so put a big "X" where the treasure is hidden!

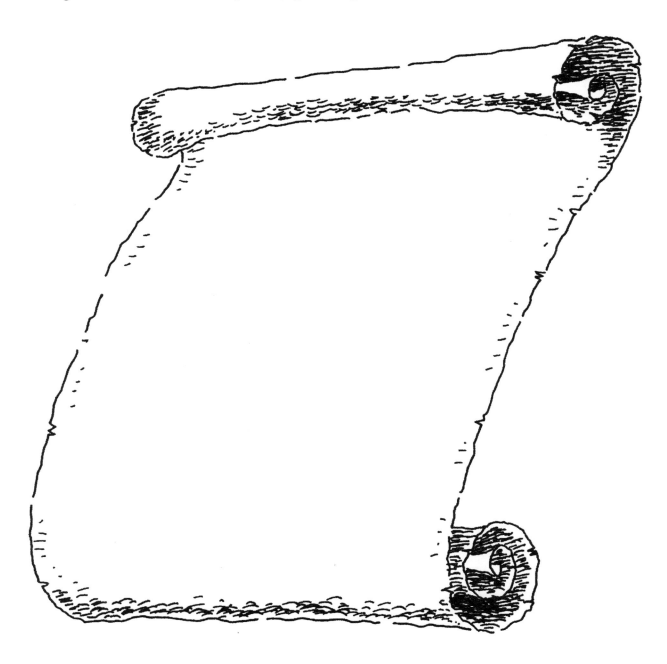

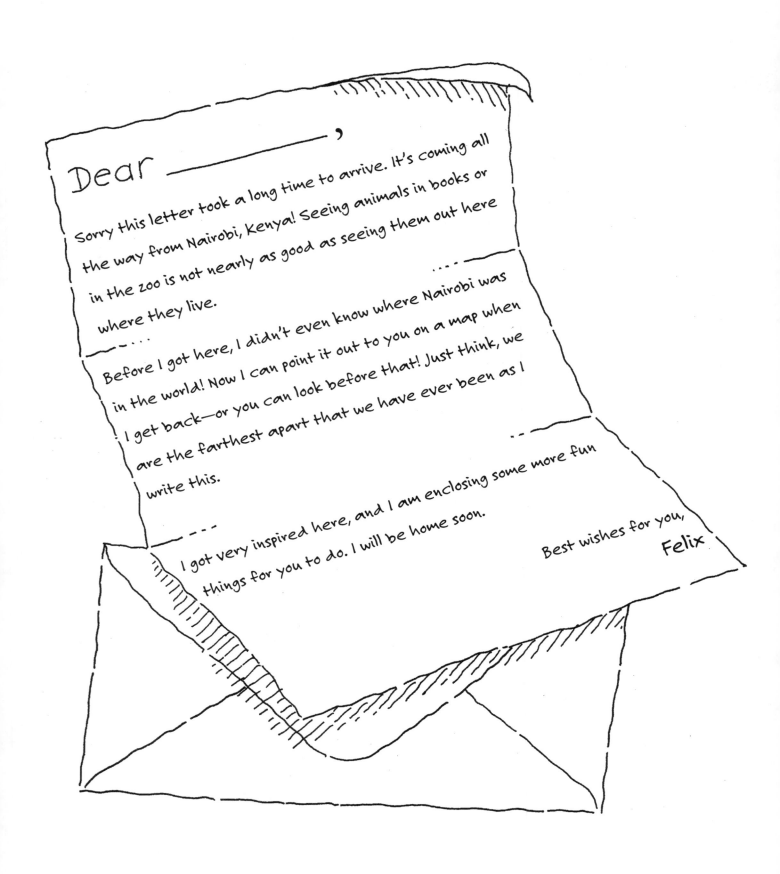

Dear _____,

Sorry this letter took a long time to arrive. It's coming all the way from Nairobi, Kenya! Seeing animals in books or in the zoo is not nearly as good as seeing them out here where they live.

Before I got here, I didn't even know where Nairobi was in the world! Now I can point it out to you on a map when I get back—or you can look before that! Just think, we are the farthest apart that we have ever been as I write this.

I got very inspired here, and I am enclosing some more fun things for you to do. I will be home soon.

Best wishes for you,
Felix

NAIROBI FACTS

Country:	Kenya
Capital city:	Nairobi
Official languages:	Swahili, English
Continent:	Africa
Number of countries in Africa:	52
Nairobi's population:	1,162,189
Kenya's climate:	tropical, high humidity
Currency:	Kenyan shilling

Some historic Kenyans:
- Jomo Kenyatta (circa 1894–1978), first president of Kenya from 1964 to 1978
- Elimo Njau (1932–present), painter
- James Ngugi (1938–present), novelist

Some symbols associated with Kenya:
- wildlife such as zebras, lions, and giraffes at many national parks

Nairobi

★★★

The Detective

Read the short paragraph about Kenya. Then be a detective. Read the sentences at the bottom of the page and decide whether or not you could be in Kenya. Circle yes or no.

Kenya's capital is Nairobi. The country is on the eastern coast of Africa. Most people in Kenya speak English or Swahili, but there are many other languages spoken there, too. Kenya is crossed by the equator, an imaginary line that runs around the earth at its middle. Countries on the equator are very hot and humid. Kenya produces coffee, tea, rice, wheat, and oil. Many people visit Kenya, and like Felix, many people like to go on a safari to see animals. The country was a British colony until 1963. Today, Kenya is one of Africa's wealthiest nations.

1. You are in a country where you hear someone speaking German.
   Could you be in Kenya?   YES   NO

2. You are in a country where zebras and elephants live.
   Could you be in Kenya?   YES   NO

3. You are in a country where many people snow ski.
   Could you be in Kenya?   YES   NO

4. You are in a country where trucks drive by carrying coffee beans.
   Could you be in Kenya?   YES   NO

5. You are in a country that does not touch the ocean.
   Could you be in Kenya?   YES   NO

solution on page 266

Pack Lightly

These are all of the things that Sophie plans to take on her trip to Nairobi. Her mother told her that she is bringing too much. She won't be able to carry it all onto the airplane. Find the items that Sophie won't need in Nairobi and circle them. Her mother will be so happy that you helped Sophie pack lightly!

solution on page 266

★★

Say It Another Way

Although many people in Nairobi speak English, Sophie became friends with a girl who speaks Swahili, a language common on the eastern coast of Africa. Sophie wants to make her statements and questions into **pictographs**, or drawings and symbols that can be understood by someone no matter what language he or she speaks.

You may have seen some pictographs like these in airports or restaurants:

Below are the sentences that Sophie wants to translate into pictographs. Draw a pictograph for each sentence. Not every word has to be represented by a picture. There are no right or wrong answers!

I live in a house in America.   I love to play with my rabbit friend Felix.

Felix visited Kenya a year ago.   I am happy that we are friends.

★★★

Can You Describe Kenya?

When Sophie returned from her visit to Kenya, she made a list of adjectives to describe the country to her family. She wants you to write a synonym, an antonym, and a rhyming word for each word she used. A **synonym** is a word that has a similar meaning. An **antonym** is a word that has the opposite meaning. There can be more than one answer for each category. The first one is done for you.

ADJECTIVE	SYNONYM	ANTONYM	RHYMING WORD
sunny	bright	cloudy	funny
hot			
flat			
dry			
pretty			
fun			

Draw a picture below of what you think Kenya looks like based on Sophie's adjectives.

solution on page 266

★

Slide Show

Sophie wanted to show her family the pictures she took of the animals while she was in Nairobi. She made a slide show. Below are the slides, but you need to draw the animals.

That is a tall giraffe!
Even the baby has a long neck.

Elephants look very friendly.

Lions are handsome,
but dangerous.

These zebras show that black
and white is always in fashion.

★★★

Sunset Over Kenya

Kenya has beautiful sunsets. Sophie could not believe how many wonderful colors she saw in the sky. She wants to use vivid words to describe these colors. Can you think of other words for each of the colors below? These are called **shades**. Write them on the lines. Give examples of things that are each color. Part of the first one is done for you. Then decorate this page any way you want, but try to use a lot of the colors and shades listed.

	DIFFERENT SHADES OF THIS COLOR	THINGS THAT ARE THIS COLOR
BLACK	ebony	licorice, crows
BLUE		
GREEN		
PURPLE		
RED		
WHITE		
YELLOW		

solution on page 267

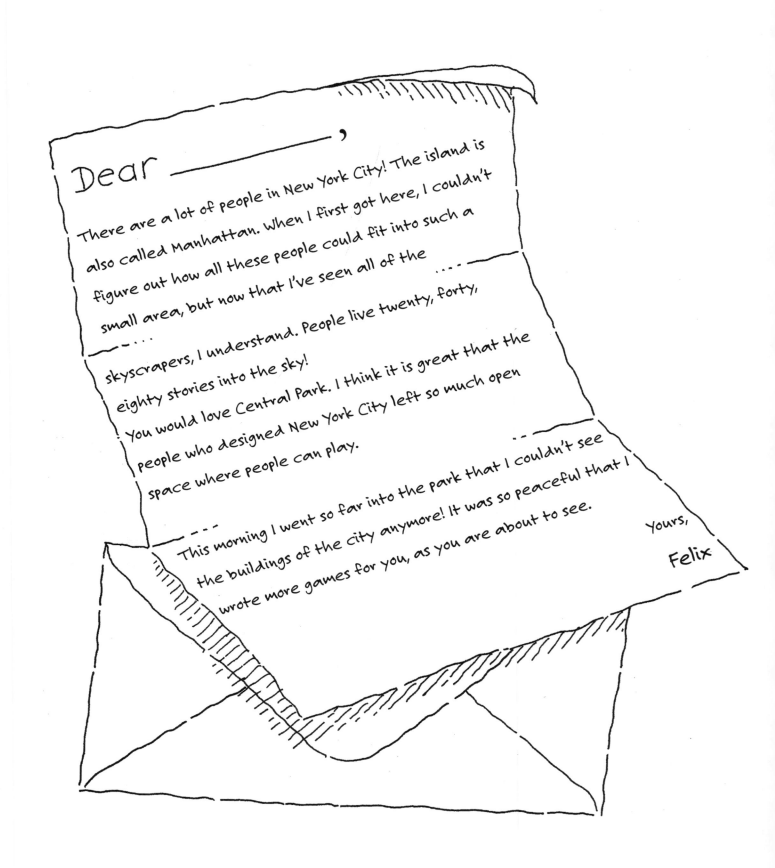

Dear _____,

There are a lot of people in New York City! The island is also called Manhattan. When I first got here, I couldn't figure out how all these people could fit into such a small area, but now that I've seen all of the skyscrapers, I understand. People live twenty, forty, eighty stories into the sky!

You would love Central Park. I think it is great that the people who designed New York City left so much open space where people can play.

This morning I went so far into the park that I couldn't see the buildings of the city anymore! It was so peaceful that I wrote more games for you, as you are about to see.

Yours,

Felix

NEW YORK CITY FACTS

Country: United States of America

Capital city
of the U.S.:   Washington, D.C.

Official language: English

Continent: North America

Number of countries
in North America: 24 (including Central America)

New York City's
population: 7,352,700

New York City's
climate: humid summers, often severely cold winters

Currency: U.S. dollar

Some historic Americans: • Betsy Ross (1752–1836), maker of first American flag
                             • Abraham Lincoln (1809–1865), 16th president of the United
                               States from 1861 to 1865, issued the Emancipation Proclamation
                               to free the slaves
                             • Clara Barton (1821–1912), organizer of the American Red Cross
                             • Thomas Edison (1847–1931), inventor of the record player, light
                               bulb, and electric typewriter, among other things
                             • Martin Luther King, Jr. (1929–1968), civil rights leader

Some symbols associated
with New York City:

• Empire State Building   • Statue of Liberty
• Rockefeller Center   • Times Square
• St. Patrick's Cathedral   • Broadway
• Wall Street   • Central Park

★★★

The Apple's Core

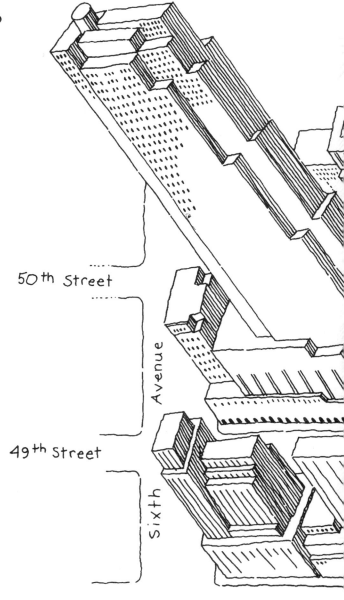

This is an isometric drawing of midtown Manhattan. An **isometric drawing** is another way to say a three-dimensional map in which the buildings don't look smaller as they get farther away like they do in real life. (If you look at a photograph of a city street, you'll see how the buildings in the distance, even those that are very big, appear to be getting smaller. This is called **perspective**.)

This isometric drawing shows portions of Madison Avenue, Fifth Avenue, and Sixth Avenue (the Avenue of the Americas). You can see Sophie standing on Madison Avenue. She is supposed to meet Felix, but he didn't tell her exactly where. Instead, he left her the clues below. By using the clues, you can help Sophie find out where she must go, then draw a line through the streets to get her there.

CLUES

1. The place you want to go does not have pointy towers.
2. You will not have to tip your head way back to see the top of this place.
3. The weight of the world is not on the shoulders of the place you are looking for.
4. You know how much Felix likes to ice skate!

Where is Felix telling Sophie to go?

_____

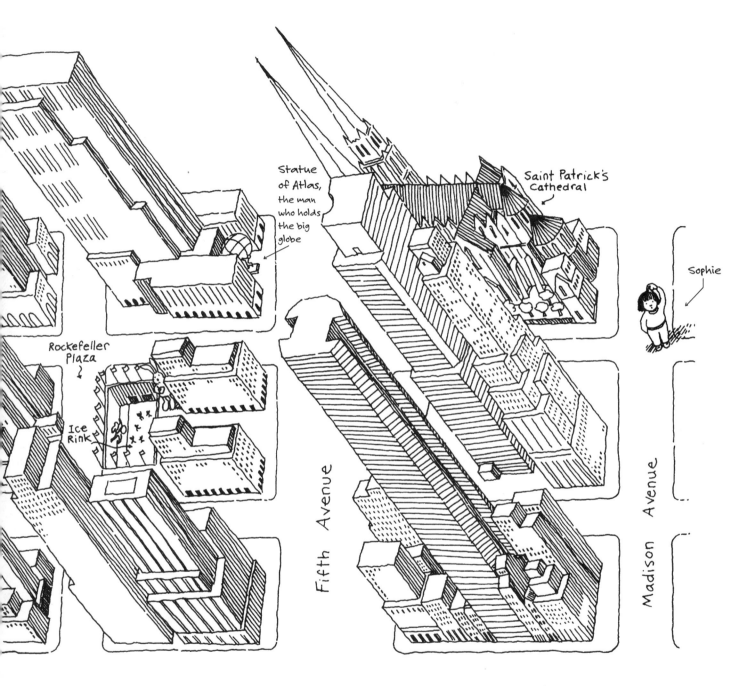

BONUS: Why is this page called "The Apple's Core"?

solution on
page 267

★
When New York Was Really New

This is a list of words that have to do with the history of New York. A short explanation of each word is given. All of the words are hidden somewhere in the letter grid below, either across or down. Circle them. Each word appears only once.

AMSTERDAM — Many of the first people to come to New York from Europe were from Amsterdam, a city in Holland. New York was originally called New Amsterdam.

HUDSON — The Hudson River is in New York. Henry Hudson was the navigator who sailed there.

ALGONQUIAN — This is a group of Native Americans. Some of them lived on what is now Manhattan Island.

DUTCH — The first people to settle in New York were Dutch (from Holland).

WALL — The Dutch built a wall in lower Manhattan to defend themselves against the Native Americans. This is how Wall Street got its name!

ENGLISH — The people who took New York from the Dutch were English.

EMPIRE — The Empire State Building was built in 1931.

```
S  D  U  T  C  H  E  V  A  P
X  R  R  W  L  C  W  O  I  B
A  E  M  P  I  R  A  X  F  H
M  D  N  P  N  C  L  M  N  Z
S  U  D  E  N  G  L  I  S  H
T  T  V  S  O  D  O  K  E  U
E  G  A  M  S  T  E  E  M  D
R  W  Y  W  A  U  M  M  U  S
D  D  J  Y  C  E  X  P  R  O
A  L  G  O  N  Q  U  I  A  N
M  O  I  T  R  E  A  R  Y  Q
Z  H  U  D  S  T  H  E  K  S
```

solution on page 267

Lady Liberty

The Statue of Liberty was given to the United States by France in 1886. It serves as a symbol of universal freedom, and it stands in the middle of New York Harbor to welcome everyone to America. Think back to 1886 when the statue was constructed. How did they make it?

Below are two drawings, one of the right side and one of the left side of the Statue of Liberty. Draw the other half of each picture.

★

Journey to Central Park

Felix is spending a busy day in New York's Central Park. Central Park is a large piece of land right in the middle of Manhattan. It is an open space where everyone can play, and no one is allowed to put big buildings there. Look what Felix can do in the park!

Circle the Central Park activity you think Felix likes best.

Color the activity you would have the most fun doing.

Next Stop: Museum of Natural History

Let's take a trip to the Museum of Natural History in New York City. The museum has world-famous exhibits of dinosaurs, whale skeletons, meteorites, spiders, gems, and human cultures. This is a picture of one of the rooms in the museum.

All of the things shown belong here—except one. Circle the object that does not belong. What is the name of that object? (HINT: See page 59 or 150.)_____

solution on page 267

ENVIRONMENT

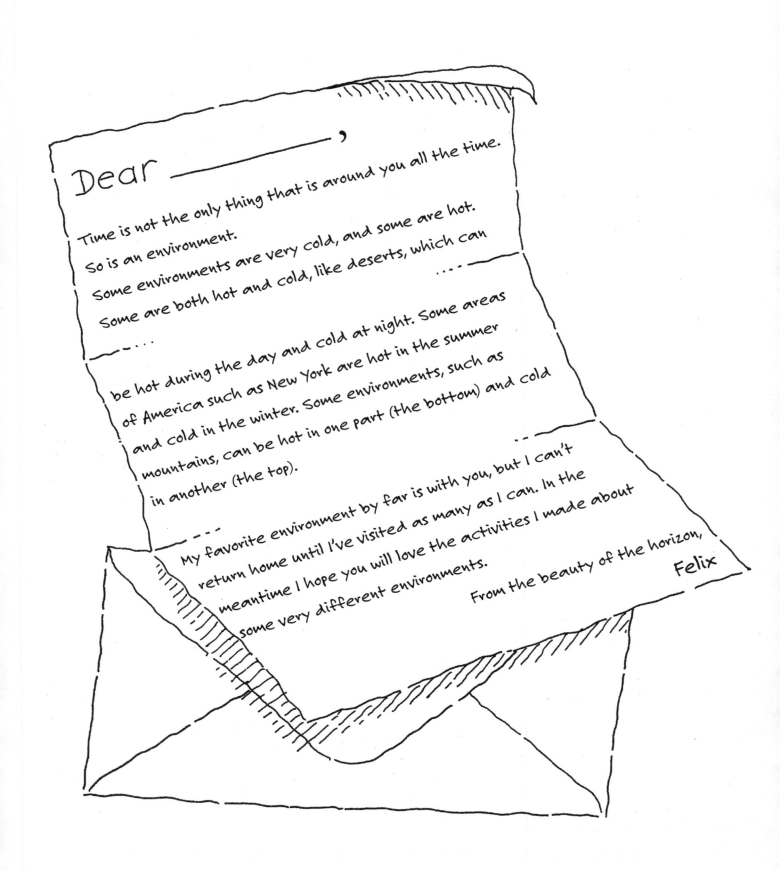

Dear _____,

Time is not the only thing that is around you all the time. So is an environment. Some environments are very cold, and some are hot. Some are both hot and cold, like deserts, which can be hot during the day and cold at night. Some areas of America such as New York are hot in the summer and cold in the winter. Some environments, such as mountains, can be hot in one part (the bottom) and cold in another (the top).

My favorite environment by far is with you, but I can't return home until I've visited as many as I can. In the meantime I hope you will love the activities I made about some very different environments.

From the beauty of the horizon,

Felix

ENVIRONMENT FACTS

Terms:

- living thing — animal, plant, or microorganism
- environment — surroundings of a living thing
- biosphere — the part of the Earth where living things can survive (from the bottom of the ocean to about six miles [ten kilometers] into the sky)
- climate — weather for an area over a long period of time
- habitat — natural home of an animal or plant
- ecosystem — area, such as a lake or a forest, where living things interact with their environment
- ecology — study of living things and their environment
- biome — large ecosystem with similar living things and climate

Number of biomes: 9

BIOME	DESCRIPTION	ANIMALS	EXAMPLE
polar tundra	covered in ice and snow, no trees	lemming, polar bear, tern, walrus, seal	the Arctic (North Pole)
taiga	region south of tundra, some trees, small plants	moose, caribou, bald eagle, ermine	northern Canada
temperate forest	rain anytime, variety of trees (pine, oak, birch)	bear, centipede, deer, owl, skunk	northwest United States
tropical rain forest	heavy rain, hot, humid, lots of trees and vines	jaguar, sloth, toucan, tree frog, python	Brazil
desert	almost no rain, very hot, often cold at night	camel, scorpion, Gila monster, gerbil	Mongolia and north China (Gobi)
grasslands	a lot of grass, very dry and hot, few trees	lion, giraffe, bison, ostrich, zebra	Africa
mountain	grassland or forest at bottom, tundra at top	condor, marmot, snow leopard, panda	Europe (Alps)
wetlands	swampy, fresh or saltwater, lots of plants	alligator, manatee, heron, otter, duck	Florida (Everglades)
ocean	cold, deep water, undersea mountains	fish, octopus, eel, plankton, whale	Indian Ocean

There are other variations of these biomes, but these are the basic groups.

★★

Follow Your Heart

Draw a heart on each picture that is a living thing. However, if it is a living thing, but one that does *not* have a heart, circle it.

ostrich

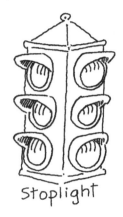

Stoplight

Sophie

flower

doll

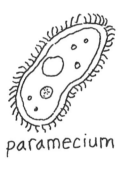

paramecium

apple tree

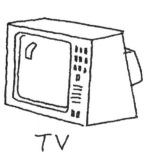

TV

solution on page 268

Take Me Home

During his travels, Felix met six other animals that had gotten lost a long way from home. Draw a line between each animal and its home environment.

solution on page 268

★★

Polar Opposites

Write the opposite for each of the polar words or phrases. The opposite can be an action, a place, or a description. One is done already.

POLAR WORD OR TERM	OPPOSITE
tip of the iceberg	bottom of the iceberg
the North Pole	
winter	
small variety of animals	
white	
water freezing to ice	

This is a picture of a friendly polar bear. Although they often look cute, polar bears can be quite mean if they are hungry or bothered. Draw the polar bear when he is the opposite of friendly—angry. Luckily, it's just a picture!

solution on page 269

Ice Breaker

A **glacier** is a large mass of ice moving slowly over land. The pieces that break off and fall into the ocean are called **icebergs**. Although they can be very big, icebergs are sometimes hard to see, which makes them very dangerous to ships. Usually you can see only a little bit (about 10 percent) of an iceberg. Most of it, the other 90 percent, is underwater.

Only one of these four icebergs could have come from this particular glacier. The rest do not fit. Circle the iceberg that just broke off.

solution on page 269

Taiga Party

The taiga is the area just south of the tundra in Canada, Europe, and Asia. Taiga is a Russian word meaning "swamp forest."

Many trees grow in the taiga, including cedar, pine, spruce, and birch. Although it is the largest land biome, it has fewer animals than other types of forests because it gets quite cold. However, it is not as cold as the tundra. Some of the animals that live there are the bald eagle, the wolverine, the snowshoe rabbit, the red fox, the moose, the Canada goose, and the ermine. That's quite a mix.

Draw a picture of these animals gathering in the taiga.

The Temperate Society

Areas that have cold winters and warm summers are called **temperate**. There are several types of temperate forests.

One type is the **deciduous** forest, which contains trees that lose their leaves in winter. These trees usually have flat leaves. Examples are oak, maple, and elm trees.

Another type is the **evergreen**, or **coniferous**, forest, which contains trees that remain green all year long. These trees usually have leaves that look like green needles, and they are more common where it is colder. Examples are pine, fir, and spruce trees.

There is even such a thing as a temperate rain forest.

In many temperate forests, squirrels bury acorns to eat in the winter, but they do not find them all. There are five acorns hidden on this page. Find and circle them. Also, there are five acorns hidden on other pages in this book! Find and circle them.

solution on page 269

★★★

Raking the Elaves

Felix collected many leaves from his visits to forests—flat leaves from a deciduous forest and needle leaves from an evergreen forest. But on his way home to show the beautiful leaves to Sophie, he dropped his bag, and the leaves scattered on the ground.

You can see that each leaf is marked with a letter. Write the names of six types of trees by rearranging the letters to spell them. Use each letter only once.

HINTS:
- three trees are deciduous and must be spelled using only deciduous leaves
- three trees are evergreen and must be spelled using only evergreen leaves

The deciduous trees

1. _____
2. _____
3. _____

The evergreen trees

1. _____
2. _____
3. _____

BONUS:

Why is this activity called "Raking the Elaves?" _____

solution on page 270

Life in the Rain Four-est

Tropical rain forests have a very specific climate and appearance.

Here are four lists of words. Only one of these lists has words that could all be used to describe a tropical rain forest. Circle the correct list.

1. rainy, cold, green, filled with animals
2. rainy, hot, green, filled with animals
3. rainy, hot, green, without animals
4. dry, hot, green, filled with animals

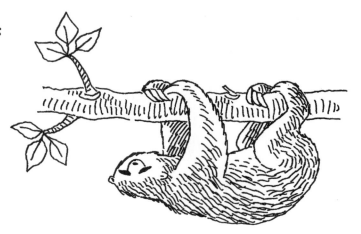

Here are four more lists of words. Only one of these lists has animals that all live in a tropical rain forest. Circle the correct list.

1. orangutans, toucans, tree frogs, harpy eagles
2. army ants, spider monkeys, sloths, penguins
3. army ants, bison, sloths, toucans
4. raccoons, spider monkeys, army ants, jaguars

The world has seven continents. Write four of them that have tropical rain forests.
HINT: You probably live on one.

1. _____
2. _____
3. _____
4. _____

solution on page 270

★★

Layer Up

Tropical rain forests have more different types of animals and plants than all other ecosystems on Earth combined. How do they all fit? Easy—they don't all live on the ground. Actually, most live near the top.

The tropical rain forest usually has five layers:

1. **emergent layer**—a few very tall trees tower above everything else, except flying birds
2. **canopy**—the tops of most of the trees, where many climbing mammals hang out
3. **lower canopy**—darker and cooler than the canopy, where snakes often slither
4. **understory**—young trees and shrubs, where tree frogs stick to leaves
5. **ground**—little sunlight, where the largest animals hunt for food

Somehow five tropical rain forest animals have wandered into the wrong layer. Draw an arrow from each animal to the layer where it is usually found.

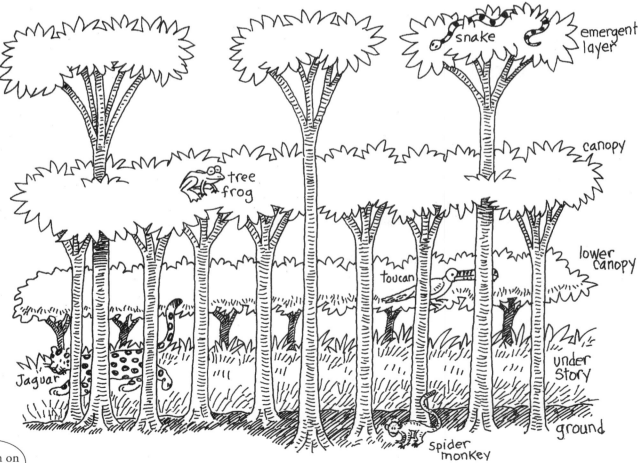

solution on page 271

★★★

Desert Crossings

What makes a region a desert? Hot temperatures? Tropical rain forests are hot, and they're not deserts. Sand? Beaches are sandy, and they're not deserts.

A desert gets less than 4 inches (10 cm) of rain a year. Of course, deserts are hot and sandy, but that is not what is unique about them.

Read each desert question. Write the answer next to the same number in the grid. Write across, and use one letter per box. The first letter from each answer is already written for you.

1. What biome is defined by how little annual rainfall it gets? (6 letters)
2. What lizard "monster" lives in the southwest desert area of America? (4 letters)
3. In what part of their bodies do camels store fat? (4 letters)
4. What type of desert plant is covered with sharp spines? (6 letters)
5. What is the name of the small desert creature that stings with its tail? (8 letters)
6. In some deserts, where can water sometimes be found? (5 letters)

Now read down the columns. One of them hides the name of the world's largest desert. Which desert is it?_____

solution on page 271

111

★★

Australian for Fun

Much of Australia is a desert, a very dry and sandy area of land.

This is a story about Felix's adventure in the desert of Australia—but there's a problem. Some of the words were blown away in a sandstorm! Fill in the blanks with any word you like to complete the story. Then read your story to your family and friends.

"A Little Rabbit in a Big Desert"

Early in the morning, when it was not yet so hot, Felix started walking across the desert of Australia. He was headed toward the airport so he could fly home to Sophie.

On his head, he wore his favorite _____. He also carried his bag, which was filled with _____ and _____. The only other thing he brought was a gift he got for Sophie in Melbourne, a big Australian city. The gift was a _____, and Felix knew she would love it.

Before long, the _____ sun was high in the sky. It looked like a big _____. Felix was feeling _____ and a bit lonely, too. Suddenly a gust of wind blew some sand into Felix's eyes. As he rubbed them to get the sand out, something ran past him very quickly. Felix thought it might have been a _____, but he didn't think any of those animals lived in Australia.

"I guess it was a small kangaroo," Felix said to himself.

Just as he finished removing all the sand, he saw whatever it was again. It was still _____ very fast.

"This time, it looked just like a _____! And this time, there was no _____ in my eyes!" Felix said.

One _____ later, Felix saw something that made him very happy. A whole group of rabbits appeared!

One of the rabbits said, "I did not mean to _____ you. I was just playing with my friend _____."

"That's okay," Felix said. "It's nice to see someone out here in the desert, especially _____!"

"You look lost," another rabbit said. "Where are you going?"

"To the _____," Felix said. "Do you know the way?"

"Yes. And we'll all come with you on your journey," the first rabbit said.

"That's very nice of you," Felix said. "It really is true that you can make friends anywhere, even in the _____ of Australia."

★

Grasslands Are Always Greener

Where there isn't enough rain for a forest but too much for a desert, conditions are good for a grassland.

Grasslands have different names in different parts of the world. They are called **prairies** in America, **savannas** in Africa, and **steppes** in Asia. Grasslands usually look brown in winter and bright green in summer.

The world's fastest mammal (cheetah), tallest mammal (giraffe), and most famous striped horse (zebra) all live in grasslands.

Cheetahs may be the fastest, but the others run fast too.

Cheetahs run 70 miles per hour (113 km/hr)
Giraffes run 32 miles per hour (51 km/hr)
Zebras run 40 miles per hour (64 km/hr)
Humans run only about 27 miles per hour (45 km/hr)

All three animals were in a race, and they ran so fast that their coats flew off! Draw a line between each animal and the pattern of his skin.

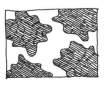

solution on page 272

113

★
Thou Shalt Not Poach

Like many other animals in other ecosystems, the wildlife in the grasslands is in constant danger—not just from each other, but from humans. In some places, grazing areas have been converted to agricultural fields, forcing animals away. Some animals are killed for food. Others are killed for their skins or even just for sport. Illegal hunting is called **poaching**. Even the most powerful animals are powerless against guns.

Read the beginning of the story. Finish it on the lines provided. Use another sheet of paper if you need more room.

"What is the ugliest animal you've ever seen?" the man asked the boy.

"Well, maybe a rhinoceros," the boy said.

The man and the boy were in the African grasslands, where they had a good chance of seeing a rhinoceros.

"But that doesn't mean I don't like them," the boy said. "I do like them."

The man was a poacher. The people whose job it is to protect wildlife are called game wardens, and if they knew this man was there, they would tell him to leave.

"I like rhinos, too," the man said.

The boy, a member of a local tribe, was on his way home when he passed the hunter. He had seen many animals shot in the grasslands, often because people can sell certain parts of animals for money. Rhinoceros horns are often desired because they can be used for art and even for medicine.

"Why did you come here?" the boy said.

"I'm—uh, a zookeeper."

The boy had never seen a zookeeper. He had seen many hunters and poachers, and they all carried guns, like this man did. The boy had seen many dead rhinoceroses. It was always a sad sight. "So you're here to catch a rhino for the zoo?"

Just then, a rhinoceros did appear. He was walking slowly, eating grass. He looked toward the man and boy but showed no interest and went back to his lunch.

"Run along home now," the poacher said. "I have work to do."

The poacher aimed his gun at the big gray rhino. The animal was very peaceful. It didn't look so ugly to the boy anymore.

He decided to say something to the poacher.

What happens next? _____

_____

_____

Mountain View

Sophie is walking on a mountain trail. Three animals observe her, and each sees her in a different way.

Golden Eagle

Sophie

Mountain Gorilla

Woodchuck

Next to each view of Sophie, write which of the three mountain animals is looking at her. Each animal is used once.

_____   _____   _____

solution on page 272

★
High Altitude Jumble

Read the questions about mountains. You may know the answer on your own, or you can unscramble the word after each question to find it.

1. The **tree line** is the height on a mountain above which trees cannot grow because it is too windy and _____. CLOD

2. When a _____ erupts, lava shoots up, and steam and gas escape from the opening in the Earth . COOLVAN

3. The world's tallest mountain is _____ in the Himalayas in Asia. SEVTREE

4. There is less _____, as you go higher up a mountain, making it more difficult to breathe. YEOGNX

5. A _____ is a bird that frequently looks in the mountains for animal carcasses to eat. TRUELUV

6. _____ is a word derived from the Alps mountain range that means "relating to high mountains." NEPALI

solution on pages 272–273

Slippery When Wetland

Wetlands are places where the ground is covered by shallow water. There are three types:

1. A **swamp** is a waterlogged forest
2. A **marsh** is a wet grassland
3. A **bog** is a wet peatland (an area where dead plants pile up very quickly)

Many birds live in wetlands because most predators cannot live there. Large animals would sink into the soft, muddy ground.

One of the most lovable animals living in wetlands is the manatee. Manatees are gentle, fat, plant-eating mammals whose closest relative is the elephant. In centuries past, sailors who had been at sea too long often mistook manatees in the distance for mermaids!

In this group of silhouettes, find and circle the manatee. Then circle the mermaid. Do they look alike?

solution on page 273

★★

Deep, Very Deep

Oceans are huge bodies of salt water that cover more than 70 percent of the Earth's surface. The Atlantic, Pacific, and Indian are the three main oceans, and they are all connected.

Oceans are divided into two living regions, the water itself (the **pelagic habitat**) and the ocean floor (the **benthic habitat**). When you think of ocean animals, you probably first think of sharks and whales, but most of the ocean's animals live on the floor.

Draw each of these animals in either the pelagic habitat (water) or the benthic habitat (floor), depending on where it lives.

sperm whale

squid

swordfish

jellyfish

lobster

sea anemone

BONUS:
manta ray

solution on page 273

Rain Forests of the Sea

Many people think coral is just rock—but it's alive! When thousands of small marine animals called **polyps** attach to the hard skeletons of other polyps in a concentrated area, a colorful coral reef is formed. Coral reefs grow only in warm, shallow water.

Starfish, sea urchins, sea slugs, and many kinds of fish are some of the many animals that live on or around coral reefs. Because so many animals are found there, coral reefs have been called the "rain forests of the sea."

In the boxes below, write any words that you can make from the nine letters in the phrase CORAL REEF. A few are done for you. There is no correct number of answers. If you fill the boxes and think of more words, write them next to the boxes.

The words coral and reef don't count.

CORAL REEF

aloe		
are		
car		
care		

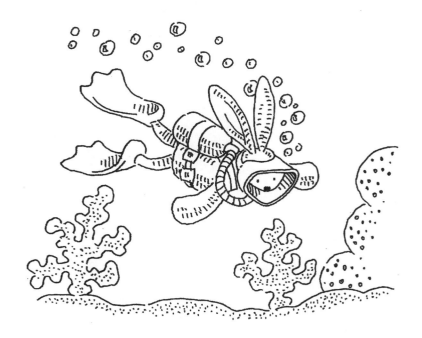

solution on page 274

15,000 B.C.E.   500 B.C.E.   900 C.E.

HISTORY

1100 C.E.   1500 C.E.   1650 C.E.

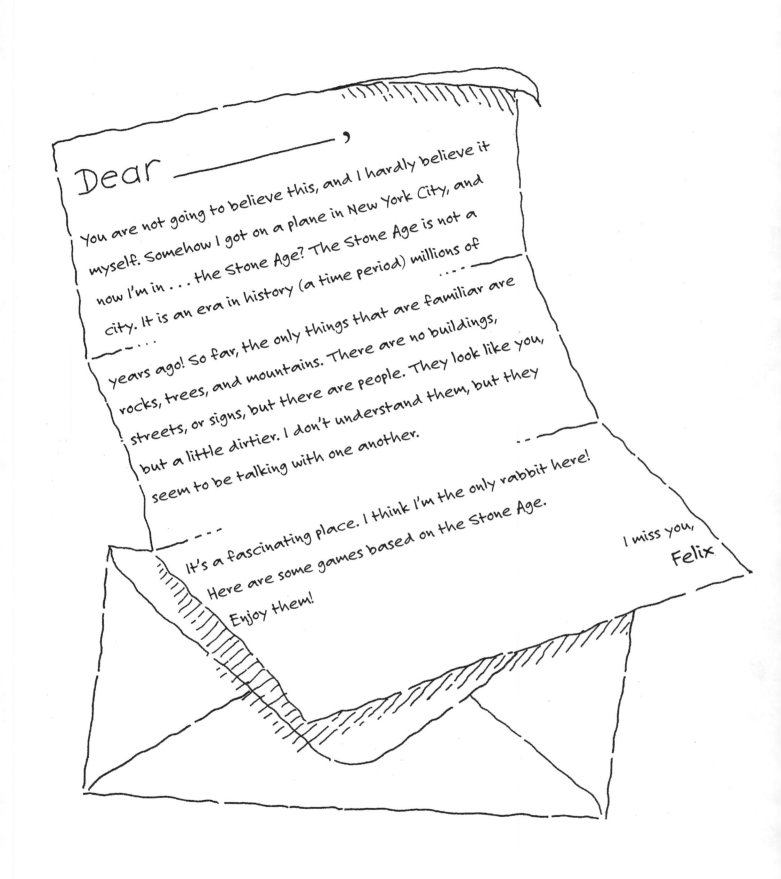

Dear ————,

You are not going to believe this, and I hardly believe it myself. Somehow I got on a plane in New York City, and now I'm in . . . the Stone Age? The Stone Age is not a city. It is an era in history (a time period) millions of years ago! So far, the only things that are familiar are rocks, trees, and mountains. There are no buildings, streets, or signs, but there are people. They look like you, but a little dirtier. I don't understand them, but they seem to be talking with one another.

It's a fascinating place. I think I'm the only rabbit here! Here are some games based on the Stone Age. Enjoy them!

I miss you,
Felix

THE STONE AGE FACTS

Dates:	circa 2,000,000 B.C.E.–8000 B.C.E.
How the era got its name:	People used stones as tools and weapons.
Location:	the entire world, although the term "Stone Age" refers to the development of people in Europe in particular

Some important advances or inventions:

- bow and arrow
- ax
- needle
- fish hook
- beads
- comb
- bow
- spear

Associated people:

- *Homo habilis* ("handy man")
- *Homo erectus* ("upright man")
- Neanderthals
- *Homo sapiens*
- *Homo sapiens sapiens* (modern human)

Symbols:

- woolly mammoths
- stone tools
- cave paintings

Wall's Well that Ends Well

In some southern European countries, historians have found art on the walls of caves. The paintings often show hunting scenes and were painted for luck. Three explorers in France found a huge underground cave with colorful paintings of horses, bears, lions, and other beasts. These paintings are at least 30,000 years old!

Draw a scene below that you would paint for luck on your own cave wall.

★★★

The First Firsts

People in the Stone Age invented a lot of important things, but often, millions of years would pass between discoveries.

Here's a list of accomplishments by early people. Put them in the order that you think they happened. Think of which events seem the most simple. Those probably came first. Think of which events seem the most hard to do. Those probably came later. Scientists think they know the right order, but we may never know for sure!

- Creating art (like sculpture and painting)
- Farming
- Living in huts
- Speaking a language
- Using animals (like dogs) as pets and helpers
- Using fire
- Using modified tools (such as blades and bone points)
- Using stone tools to get food
- Walking upright (on two feet)
- Wearing simple jewelry (beads)

In what order do you think these events happened?

1. _____
2. _____
3. _____
4. _____
5. _____
6. _____
7. _____
8. _____
9. _____
10. _____

solution on page 274

Not in Any Zoo

The woolly mammoth was a large, hairy animal with very curvy tusks. It lived during the Stone Age. Woolly mammoths are now **extinct**, which means that they are no longer alive today. However, animals that look like woolly mammoths are still alive now. The elephant is a relative of the woolly mammoth!

Other animals have become extinct, too. Some are in danger of becoming extinct even today. There are a lot of animals that we know about but that no person has ever actually seen, like dinosaurs. Because they are extinct, we only know about dinosaurs from their bones. Animals become extinct for different reasons. Some are killed off by people, some run out of food, and some are not able to handle changes in the weather.

Imagine an extinct animal and draw its picture. Be creative. Your animal can look any way you want. It does not have to look like something that exists today.

What is the name of your extinct animal? _____

Why is your animal extinct? _____

★★★

Sticks and Stones Can Break My Bones, but Words Will Tell the Future

The people who lived during the Stone Age were probably the first people who lived on this planet. They did not write with the letters of any alphabet that we use today. Scientists think people communicated with each other then, but they don't know how.

Pretend that you found a list that a cave person left and that you know how to translate it. You see that this cave person was guessing about the future. He wrote five things that he thought would happen long after the cave people had disappeared.

What five things did this cave person predict? Are his predictions correct? Write "yes" or "no."

	PREDICTION	IS IT CORRECT?
1.		
2.		
3.		
4.		
5.		

If you could go back and visit people from the Stone Age, what five things about the present would you want to tell them?

1.
2.
3.
4.
5.

★

Tool Time

Early people often needed nothing more than a stone shaped a certain way to use as a tool. Below is a list of five tools and a picture of five different rocks. Draw a line between the name of the tool and the rock that is the right shape to be used as that tool.

knife

ax

hammer

spear tip

bowl

solution on
page 275

128

Hot on the Trail

Can you tell what type of animal this caveman is following by the footprints? Write your guess below. Draw in the caveman's footprints, too.

What is he following? _____ Draw the animal below.

solution on page 275

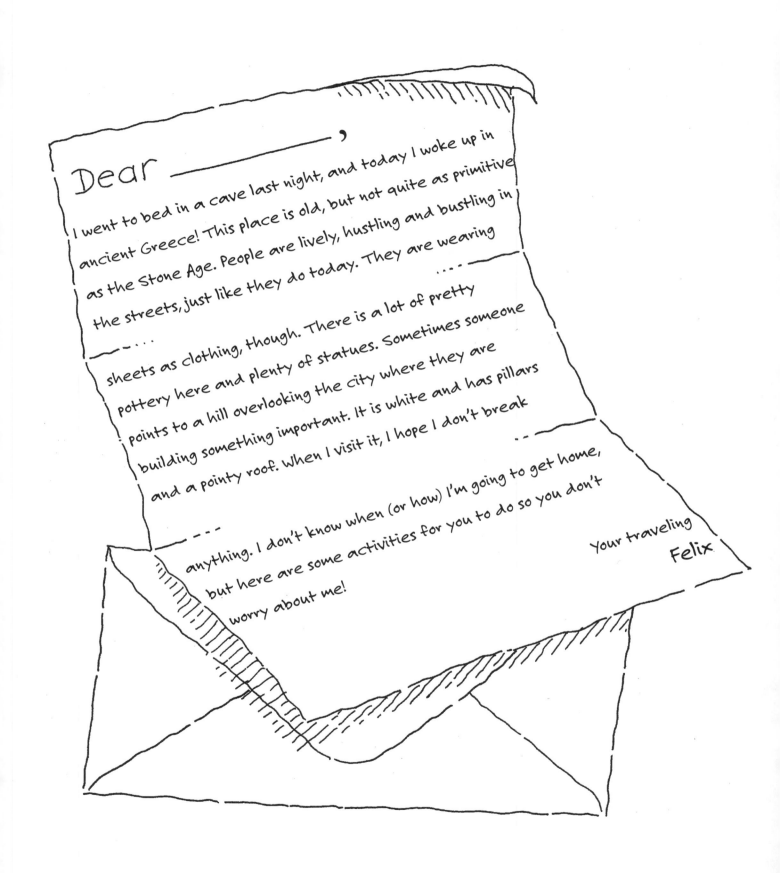

Dear _____,

I went to bed in a cave last night, and today I woke up in ancient Greece! This place is old, but not quite as primitive as the Stone Age. People are lively, hustling and bustling in the streets, just like they do today. They are wearing sheets as clothing, though. There is a lot of pretty pottery here and plenty of statues. Sometimes someone points to a hill overlooking the city where they are building something important. It is white and has pillars and a pointy roof. When I visit it, I hope I don't break anything. I don't know when (or how) I'm going to get home, but here are some activities for you to do so you don't worry about me!

Your traveling
Felix

ANCIENT GREECE FACTS

Dates: circa 800 B.C.E.–336 B.C.E. (the Archaic Period
                      and the Classical Age)

Location: Europe

Some important advances
or inventions:
- democracy (a form of government in
  which the people can participate)
- advanced forms of writing

Associated people:
- Pythagoras (circa 582–550 B.C.E.), mathematician
- Pericles (circa 495–429 B.C.E.), statesman who had the
  Parthenon built
- Socrates (circa 469–399 B.C.E.), Plato (428–347 B.C.E.), and
  Aristotle (384–322 B.C.E.), philosophers and teachers

Symbols:
- Olympics
- Parthenon (the temple on a hill overlooking Athens)
- Greek gods
- fine pottery

★★

Thrill of Victory

In 776 B.C.E., the first Olympic Games were held in Greece. The first modern Olympic Games were held in Athens, Greece, in 1896.

Here are nine Olympic athletes: three discus throwers, three javelin throwers, and three shot putters. A **discus** is usually made of wood; it looks like and is thrown like a Frisbee.™ A **javelin** is also made of wood, and it looks like and is thrown like a spear. A **shot** is a heavy metal ball about the size of a grapefruit.

Each row of three athletes below has something in common. For example, everyone in the first row across is a discus thrower.

	COLUMN 1	COLUMN 2	COLUMN 3
ROW 1			
ROW 2			
ROW 3			

Find the similarities and write them below.

ROW 1:   all discus throwers   COLUMN 1: _____

ROW 2:   _____   COLUMN 2: _____

ROW 3:   _____   COLUMN 3: _____

DIAGONAL: _____   DIAGONAL: _____
(top left to bottom right)   (top right to bottom left)

solution on page 275

Lost among the Ruins

In Athens, you just found a stone tablet with some writing on it. A **tablet** is a surface, often made of stone, wood, metal, or paper, on which people write. Unfortunately, because this tablet is so old, most of the words have worn away over the years.

Pretend you are a historian. It is up to you to figure out what is written on the tablet below. You see that the first words are "The People of Greece. . . ." Write the rest of the tablet. The following phrases can be read as well. Be sure to include them.

WE WILL BUILD • FOR CENTURIES • SECRET WEALTH • A GREAT NATION

The phrases may appear in any order. There are no right or wrong answers.

Family Reunion

Have you heard the names Aphrodite, Poseidon, or Zeus? Today, they are known as characters in mythology, but to the ancient Greeks, they were members of the family of gods that they worshipped. The Greeks used these gods to explain things in nature. Each god was responsible for protecting a specific part of life. Felix learned all about them on his trip to Athens.

Listed below are a few of the gods that the Greeks worshipped. You may have seen or heard some of these names before. Some of these words have been used to name ships or spacecraft.

- **Aphrodite:** goddess of love and beauty
- **Apollo:** god of light, music, and healing; Artemis's twin brother
- **Artemis:** goddess of the moon; Apollo's twin sister
- **Hera:** goddess of women and marriage; Zeus's wife
- **Hermes:** messenger of the gods
- **Pan:** god of the forest and wild animals
- **Poseidon:** god of the sea
- **Zeus:** leader of the gods; Hera's husband

Draw a family reunion of the ancient Greek gods below. Add a new one if you want, name him or her, and write what aspect of the world this god or goddess protects.

Bringing Things into Focus

Below are two photographs that Felix took in ancient Greece, but neither one came out very well. Sophie is disappointed.

Here is a picture of Felix trying to throw the discus. But Felix is too small—someone took the picture from too far away!
Draw the picture from a closer viewpoint so that Sophie can see it better.

Here is a picture of Felix in front of the Parthenon, but it is blurry!
Draw the picture more clearly so that Sophie can see it better.

Ask a Smart Question...

The ancient Greeks were curious people. They did not simply accept things. They asked a lot of questions to understand why things were the way they were. Some of the people who asked those questions are some of the most respected thinkers who ever lived. Socrates, Plato, and Aristotle are three such men from ancient Greece.

Socrates believed he could teach the difference between right and wrong. Plato said that telling stories is the most important part of early education. Aristotle invented the encyclopedia. An **encyclopedia** is a book or a set of books that has facts and pictures about many different subjects.

Below are some words that you might find in an encyclopedia. Explain each word on the lines. Draw a picture of each word in the blank boxes. You are making a short encyclopedia.

COMPUTER

FRUIT

SCHOOL

★★

Marathon Session

A **marathon** is a long race in which people run about twenty-six miles (forty-two kilometers). In 490 B.C.E., the ancient Greeks won a battle against a group of people called the Persians at a place called Marathon. Marathon was about twenty-six miles away from Athens, which was the main city of ancient Greece. This event happened before telephones and television, so a Greek man named Pheidippides had to run the entire distance from Marathon to Athens just to tell his fellow Greeks that they had won. This is why a race of this distance is called a marathon.

Are the following distances longer or shorter than a marathon?

LONGER or SHORTER than a marathon?

1. The distance between your house and your mailbox _____

2. The distance between the Earth and the moon _____

3. The distance that you can throw a ball _____

4. The distance between Greece and New York City _____

5. The distance between the fingertips of your left and right hands when your arms are stretched out as far as they go _____

BONUS: The distance between your house and your school _____

solution on page 275

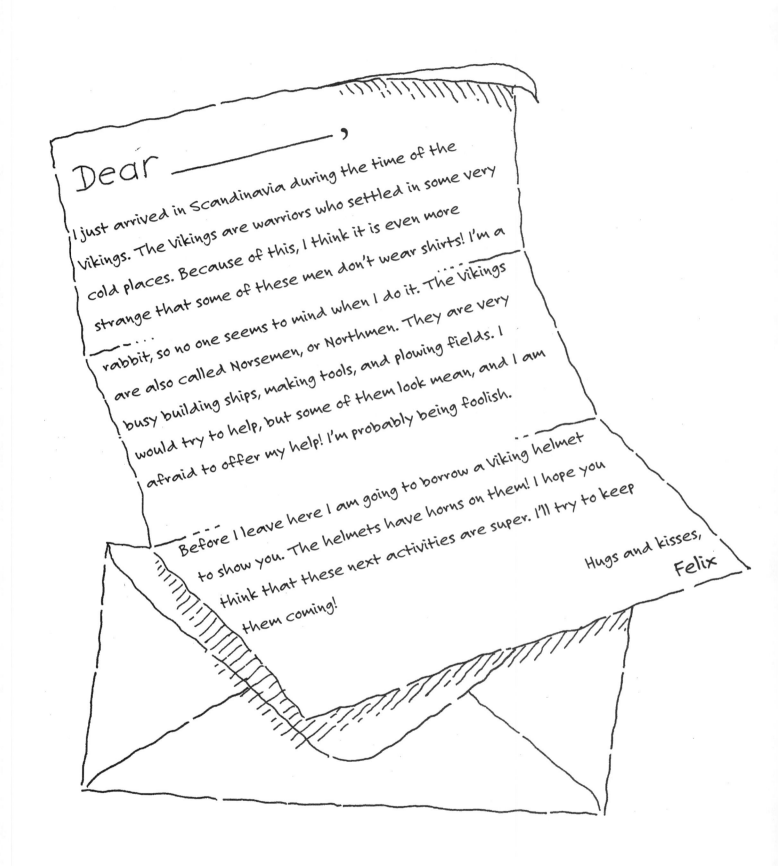

Dear _____,

I just arrived in Scandinavia during the time of the Vikings. The Vikings are warriors who settled in some very cold places. Because of this, I think it is even more strange that some of these men don't wear shirts! I'm a rabbit, so no one seems to mind when I do it. The Vikings are also called Norsemen, or Northmen. They are very busy building ships, making tools, and plowing fields. I would try to help, but some of them look mean, and I am afraid to offer my help! I'm probably being foolish.

Before I leave here I am going to borrow a Viking helmet to show you. The helmets have horns on them! I hope you think that these next activities are super. I'll try to keep them coming!

Hugs and kisses,
Felix

THE TIME OF THE VIKINGS FACTS

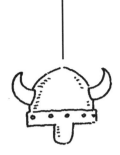

Dates: circa 700–1000

Location: Scandinavia (Norway, Sweden, and Denmark)

Some important
advances or inventions:
- the saga, a long, written story about a historical or legendary person
- the Vikings settled Iceland

Associated people:
- Eric the Red (circa 950–1000), explorer who settled Greenland circa 985
- Leif Ericsson, Eric the Red's son, who may have come to what is now Newfoundland in North America circa 1000, which was before Christopher Columbus arrived

Symbols:
- longships
- helmets with horns
- huts with thatch (straw) roofs

Dig This

You just dug up a **time capsule**, which is a box or a chest that people fill with things from their lives and then bury so that people in the future will know what life was like in the past.

This time capsule appears to be from the time of the Vikings. Inside this time capsule, draw or write the items you might find.

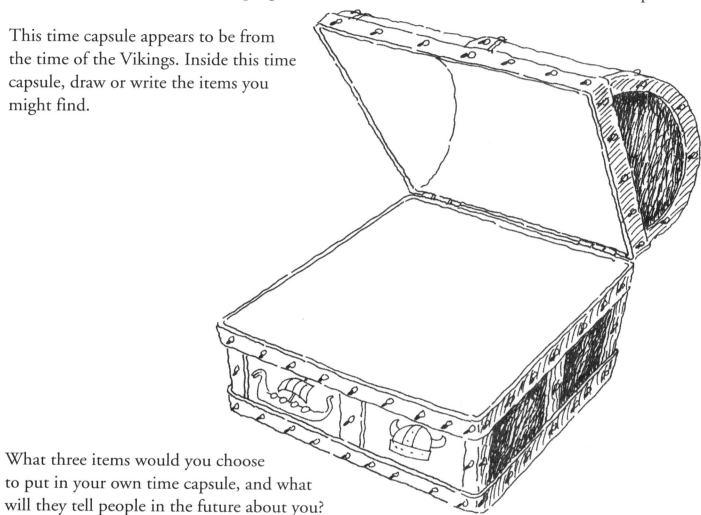

What three items would you choose to put in your own time capsule, and what will they tell people in the future about you?

ITEM	WHAT IT TELLS ABOUT YOU
1.	
2.	
3.	

In what year would you want your time capsule to be opened? _____

Why? _____

★★★

Viking Truth

Write whether each statement about the Vikings is true or false.

TRUE or FALSE

1. It is possible that Vikings came to North America as early as the year 1000, almost 500 years before Christopher Columbus. _____

2. The name of the Viking who may have come to America first is Leif Ericsson. _____

3. Leif Ericsson's Viking settlement was in Newfoundland, Canada. _____

4. Another early Viking settlement was in Orlando, Florida. _____

5. Vikings lived in Scandinavia. _____

6. Norway, Sweden, and Denmark are countries in Scandinavia. _____

7. Vikings were also called Norsemen. _____

8. Iceland is a country that the Vikings settled. _____

9. Roofs of Viking houses were made of stone. _____

10. Viking ships usually had more than ten sails. _____

solution on page 276

★★

Nothing to Fear

Vikings would carve dragons into the prows of their ships to scare their enemies. The **prow** is the front of the ship. Here are three Viking longships, but none have prows.

Draw a different prow on each of these three ships. On the lines near each ship, write why a Viking would want each one of your prow ideas for his ship.

Why would a Viking like this prow?

_____

_____

_____

Why would a Viking like this prow?

_____

_____

_____

Why would a Viking like this prow?

_____

_____

_____

★

Mirror Images

Draw the shadow of this Viking and draw the reflection of his ship in the water.
(Hold this page up to a mirror to read the trick title of this activity!)

Viking Women

Vikings were barbarians who were often violent robbers. Although they were feared all over Europe, they did some good, too. They were hard workers on the farm, they fished, they made crafts, and they built excellent ships. Viking women were also very strong. When their husbands were away, the women would take care of the farm. Unlike most women from this time in history, Viking women were allowed to own a piece of land.

Here are some activities that Viking women did. Which of the jobs would you like to do? Which jobs wouldn't you like? Circle either "would like" or "wouldn't like" next to each task.

1. Growing oats on the farm   WOULD LIKE or WOULDN'T LIKE?

2. Carving house items, like bowls   WOULD LIKE or WOULDN'T LIKE?

3. Cooking a meal   WOULD LIKE or WOULDN'T LIKE?

4. Feeding the farm animals   WOULD LIKE or WOULDN'T LIKE?

5. Making clothes   WOULD LIKE or WOULDN'T LIKE?

Which task would be your favorite?   _____

Which task would be your least favorite?   _____

What other tasks do you think you might like to do? _____

_____

_____

Ships Set Sail

Vikings lived on seacoasts, and they became expert shipbuilders. Each ship below has a mistake that would make it dangerous or difficult to sail.

Find each mistake, and write what it is on the line below each ship.

1.

_____

2.

_____

3.

_____

solution on page 276

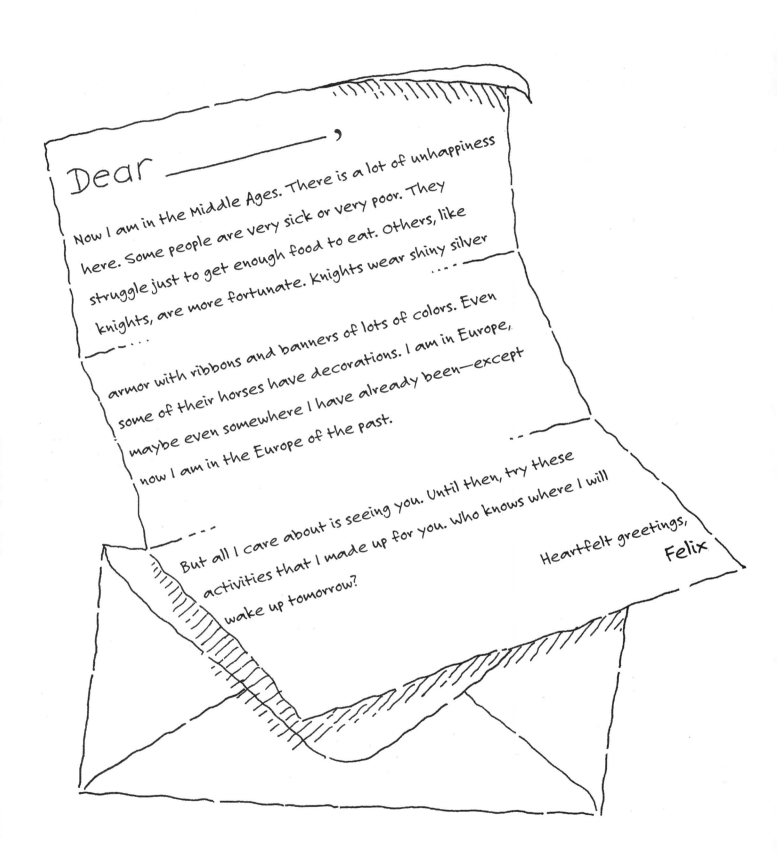

Dear _____,

Now I am in the Middle Ages. There is a lot of unhappiness here. Some people are very sick or very poor. They struggle just to get enough food to eat. Others, like knights, are more fortunate. Knights wear shiny silver armor with ribbons and banners of lots of colors. Even some of their horses have decorations. I am in Europe, maybe even somewhere I have already been—except now I am in the Europe of the past.

But all I care about is seeing you. Until then, try these activities that I made up for you. Who knows where I will wake up tomorrow?

Heartfelt greetings,

Felix

THE MIDDLE AGES FACTS

Dates: circa 476–1450

How the era got its name: It was the time between ancient Greece and Rome and the Renaissance, therefore in the middle

Location: Western Europe, including the United Kingdom (England, Scotland, Wales, Ireland), France, Germany, and Italy

Some important advances or inventions:
- mirrors
- accounting

Associated people:
- Marco Polo (circa 1254–1324), Italian traveler
- Geoffrey Chaucer (circa 1340–1400), English poet and author of *The Canterbury Tales*
- Johannes Gutenberg (circa 1400–1468), German who introduced printing with movable type to Europe

Symbols:
- castles with moats
- knights
- exploration

★★

A Hard Day's Knight

Sir Chainmail is sent off to fight in the **Crusades**, a series of religious wars that were waged roughly between the years 1000 and 1300. One night, Sir Chainmail tries another path home to his castle. Continue reading the story in the first box below, then choose where you would like to go next until you get to an ending. Then start again and try a different option—there are six complete stories in all!

❶ Sir Chainmail comes to a fork in the road. Neither path is familiar to him. He thinks that there is more moonlight on the first path, so he starts down it. But his horse whinnies and seems scared. Sir Chainmail tries to see what could be bothering her, but even in the moonlight, the path is still quite dark.
If you want Sir Chainmail to stay on the path, go to 3; if you want him to turn back and try the other path, go to 2.

❷ Sir Chainmail trusts his horse and turns back. Once on the second path, he can see someone else on a horse up ahead. The man calls out, "You there! Who are you and what is your business?"
If you want Sir Chainmail to answer the stranger, go to 4; if you think he should ignore the stranger, go to 6.

❸ Despite his horse's anxiety, Sir Chainmail stays on the path. Soon it becomes clear why his horse was frightened. A fellow knight who is weary from battle sits by the road. Sir Chainmail realizes that he is injured. "Please help me. I am hurt," the knight says.
If you think Sir Chainmail should help this other knight, go to 8; if he should not, go to 5.

❹ "I am Sir Chainmail," he says. "My business is merely to get to my castle before morning. Who are you?" The stranger answers, "I, too, am a knight, name of Sir Noblevalor. I am in search of a contest. Are you game, friend?"
If you think Sir Chainmail should fight Sir Noblevalor, go to 7; if he should not fight, go to 9.

❺ "Poor sir, though I would like to, I am too tired to be of any help, and I must get home," Sir Chainmail says. The injured man says, "A true knight would lend his assistance at any hour for anyone." "I am sorry," Sir Chainmail says. "You are right. I shall help you." "No!" the injured man says. "You did not say 'yes' right away. I do not want your help now. Go." Sir Chainmail leaves, ashamed of his behavior. Soon, he changes his mind and goes back to the knight. "I am going to help you, no matter what you say. I made a mistake, but I want to do the right thing." Sir Chainmail takes the man to his castle, where a doctor soon cures him. Before the knight leaves Sir Chainmail's castle, he says, "Thank you. I have learned not to be too proud to accept help the second time around, and you have learned to give help the first time around. We are both better for it."

The End

❻ Sir Chainmail is exhausted and says, "My business is sleep, and at this hour, yours should be, too. Farewell."

The End

❼ "I don't wish to fight you," Sir Chainmail says. The other knight says, "It is not a fight I want. I said a contest. I propose that we race to the tower where Lady Strongsmile is held prisoner and see which man rescues her first." "That seems dangerous," Sir Chainmail says. "You're afraid," Sir Noblevalor says. "No, I am not. I only said it seems dangerous. But I will go. Let us race!"

If Sir Chainmail gets to the tower first, go to 11; if Sir Noblevalor does, go to 10.

8 "I would be most happy to help you," Sir Chainmail says. "Thank you, kind stranger. I hope that I can repay you someday," the knight says. When Sir Chainmail's castle comes into view, both men see that a band of thieves waits to rob anyone who passes. "Can we can get past so many?" Sir Chainmail asks. "I know a way," the stranger says. The two knights approach the thieves. "Your coins, knights," a thief says. "We have no coins," the stranger says. "We only have this valuable gold powder." "Give it here," another thief says. The stranger hands the thief a small bag, and the thieves let them pass. "I am sorry that they took your gold, but at least we are safe," Sir Chainmail says. "Yes," the stranger says, "but they did not get any gold. I gave them a bag of sand. They were very foolish." "Thank you, stranger. You have repaid me," Sir Chainmail says. "Now we shall get you home."

The End

9 "War is all around us, and still you want more conflict. I do not like contests, and I will not fight you," Sir Chainmail says. "Fair enough,"

Sir Noblevalor says. "That is the answer for which I search. I test each man who comes this way to see if he is worthy of the title of knight. You are more than worthy of that distinction, and you and our country should be proud."

The End

10 Sir Noblevalor sees Lady Strongsmile in the window and calls to her. "Milady! I am here to free you!" "But I am not enslaved," she calls down. "This is my home!" "I see," Sir Noblevalor says, disappointed. Sir Chainmail arrives in time to hear the woman's words. "You have won, sir," he says. "But I have not rescued her," Sir Noblevalor says. "You have given me a good race and a good laugh. For that, you earned your victory."

The End

11 Sir Chainmail arrives in time to see Lady Strongsmile climbing down a rope from the tower window. "Milady, we have come to rescue you," he says. "It appears you are too late," she says. Sir Noblevalor arrives and says, "Sir, you have won!" "No, he hasn't," the woman says. "I have, for I am free. I appreciate your concern, brave knights, but I must be off. Good luck in your quest for damsels who truly are in distress, and good night!"

The End

solution on page 276

149

★★★

A Time of Growth

The Middle Ages ended when the **Renaissance** began, a time when there was a great interest in knowledge, especially art, literature, architecture, and even science. The Renaissance started in Italy but spread throughout Europe. It lasted about 300 years.

Do you think the following items would have been important during the Renaissance? Circle yes or no.

1.   Printing books

YES   NO

2.   The Mona Lisa
(a famous painting of
a woman smiling)

YES   NO

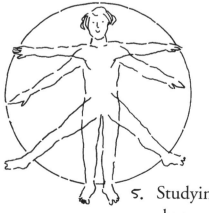

3.   Building a cathedral

YES   NO

4.   Developing railroads
and automobiles

YES   NO

5.   Studying the way the
human body works

YES   NO

solution on
page 277

Woke Up on the Wrong Side of the Moat this Morning

The castle's drawbridge is broken, and the moat is filled with dangerous animals to protect the castle. However, Felix needs to get across the water to return the minstrel's lute so the minstrel can sing for the king.

A **minstrel** is a medieval musician, and a **lute** is a medieval instrument that looks like a guitar, only rounder. The word **medieval** is used to describe anything that is from the Middle Ages.

Look at Felix's surroundings. Circle the objects in the picture that Felix can use to get across the moat.

What four ways do you see for Felix to cross the moat? Write them here.

1. _____   3. _____

2. _____   4. _____

solution on page 277

★

Survey

In 1086, the English king William I took a nationwide survey of England. A **survey** is a series of questions that someone asks to learn more about something. In this case, the survey meant that the government counted the number of people in England and found out how much land each person owned and how much that land was worth.

This is your own personal survey. It does not ask about what land you own, but it does ask about your family. Answer the survey. Now you can let other people read the survey so that they can learn more about your family.

Survey of _____'s Family
(Write your name here)

1. Where do you live?	
2. How many people do you live with?	
3. How many people who live with you are male?	
4. How many people who live with you are female?	
5. How many brothers do you have?	
6. How many sisters do you have?	
7. Are you the only child in your family, the oldest child in your family, the youngest child in your family, or somewhere in the middle?	
8. In what year were you born?	
9. What pets does your family have?	
10. What do the adults in your family do for a living?	

★★

Fair Trade

Throughout history, when people did not have any money, they would often **barter**. This means they would trade something that they had or that they could make for something else.

Pretend that you are a poor person living in the Middle Ages. You own the items in the first column. You want to buy the items in the second column. What items do you already own that you would give up for the items you want?

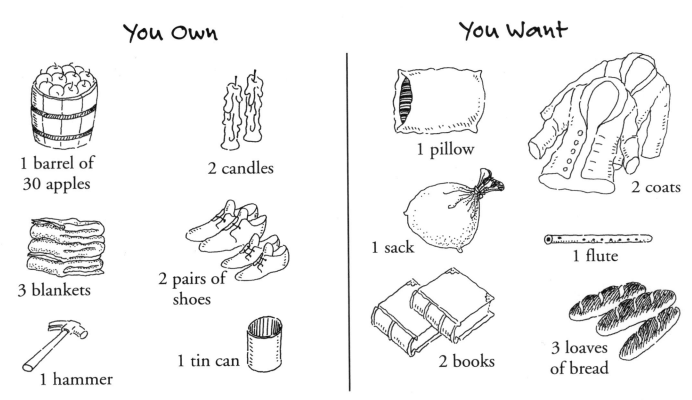

You Own | You Want

1 barrel of 30 apples

2 candles

3 blankets

2 pairs of shoes

1 hammer

1 tin can

1 pillow

1 sack

2 coats

1 flute

2 books

3 loaves of bread

Make some trades by filling in the blanks below. Think about the difference between what you want and what you need. You do not need to get everything you want. You can trade more than one item at a time, but always think about what is fair. For example, it does not seem fair to trade only one of your apples for three loaves of bread. Or does it?

I would trade _____ for _____.

I would trade _____ for _____.

I would trade _____ for _____.

I would trade _____ for _____.

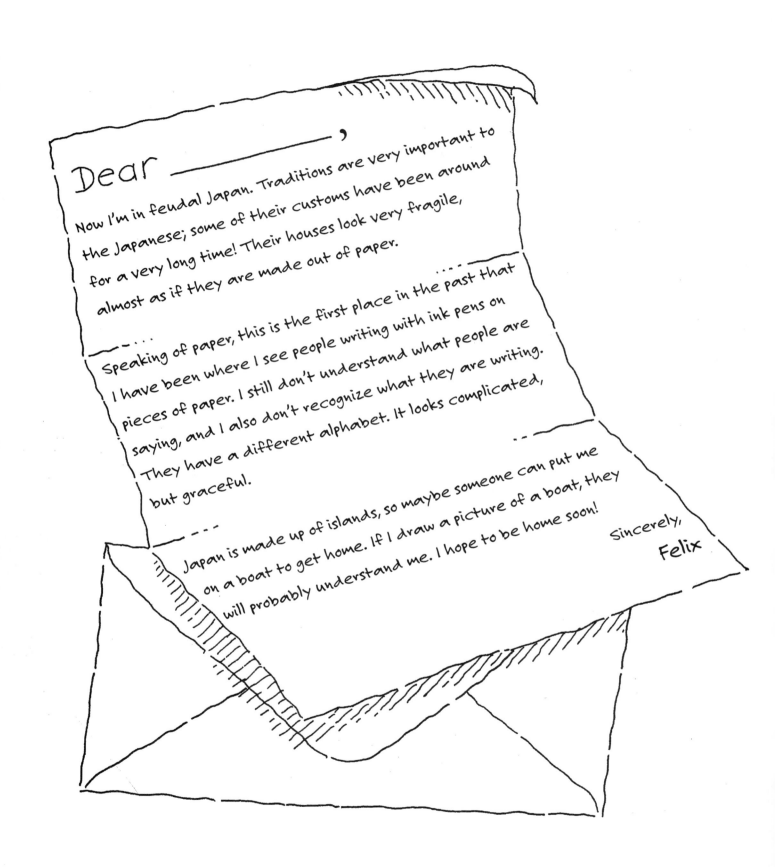

Dear _____,

Now I'm in feudal Japan. Traditions are very important to the Japanese; some of their customs have been around for a very long time! Their houses look very fragile, almost as if they are made out of paper.

Speaking of paper, this is the first place in the past that I have been where I see people writing with ink pens on pieces of paper. I still don't understand what people are saying, and I also don't recognize what they are writing. They have a different alphabet. It looks complicated, but graceful.

Japan is made up of islands, so maybe someone can put me on a boat to get home. If I draw a picture of a boat, they will probably understand me. I hope to be home soon!

Sincerely,
Felix

FEUDAL JAPAN FACTS

Dates:	circa 9th century–1867
How the era got its name:	A feudal system is when certain people work under others, called lords; in history, this system was often abused, and the poor were not treated well by the people in power.

Location:	Asia
Some important advances or inventions:	• the shogun (a military leader who served the emperor)
Associated people:	• Minamoto Yoritomo, shogun (military leader) 1192–circa 1203 • Oda Nobunaga (1534–1582), a minor feudal lord who became a political leader in 1568 • Tokugawa Ieyasu (1543–1616) became shogun in 1603 and ended feudal wars
Symbols:	• samurai • ninja

★★

Cops and Robbers

Do you think that English is the only language you speak? You probably already know some Japanese words.

NINJA

A **ninja** was a spy in feudal Japan. A ninja often used his martial arts skills for corrupt reasons. A **samurai** was a member of a group of warriors in feudal Japan. He was often involved in law enforcement and government. Each word in the following list probably has either a good connotation (like samurai) or a bad connotation (like ninja). The word **connotation** means "meaning." Or, the word may be **neutral**—neither good nor bad.

SAMURAI

Decide whether each of the following words has a good, bad, or neutral connotation. Make a ✔ or draw its picture in the box under the word you choose.

WORD	GOOD	BAD	NEUTRAL
police officer			
vitamin C			
poison			
saying "please"			
stealing			
television			

solution on page 277

★★★

Japan by the Numbers

The country of Japan is actually four main islands (Hokkaido, Honshu, Kyushu, Shikoku) and several smaller ones. Population-wise, Japan is the eighth largest country in the world. Japanese is the ninth most common language in the world.

How big is Japan in area? **Area** is the amount of land that a place fills. To find out where Japan ranks among the countries of the world in area, answer the following questions.

1. How many countries in the world have more people than Japan? _____

2. If Felix is in Japan for one week, and he writes Sophie a letter every day except for Sunday, how many letters does he write her? _____

3. Of the four main islands of Japan, how many letters are in the name of the island with the most letters? _____

4. Felix tells Sophie that when he visited feudal Japan, the people ate with "knitting needles." He was talking about chopsticks. How many chopsticks does one person need to eat? _____

5. Sophie's family is enjoying a Japanese meal. If Sophie, her dad, her mom, her two brothers, and her sister are all using chopsticks, how many total chopsticks are being used? _____

6. How many languages in the world are more common than Japanese? _____

7. The capital of Japan is Tokyo. How many letters in the word "Tokyo" are not an "o"? _____

8. Two of the islands of Japan have the same number of letters in their names. What is that number? _____

9. How many places in the past does Felix visit besides feudal Japan? _____

10. How many islands of Japan end with the letter "u"? _____

That means Japan is the _____th largest country in the world in area.

Add up the numbers above
to get Japan's rank

solution on page 278

A New Haiku for You

A **haiku** is a type of Japanese poem. It has three lines and seventeen syllables. **Syllables** are beats. The first line of a haiku has five syllables, the second has seven syllables, and the last has five syllables again. To understand the word "syllable," think of the word *Japanese*. You say this word in three beats, which means it has three syllables. First you say *Jap*, then *a*, then *nese*. Each of these three parts of the word is one syllable. Saying them a little faster, it becomes *Jap-a-nese*. Finally, you say the word normally: Japanese. Think of syllables as dividing long words into short words, even if they are nonsense words like "*nese.*"

Felix was inspired to write a haiku by his amazing trip to feudal Japan. This is what Felix's haiku looks like with every syllable in its own box. You can see that most of the words that Felix uses are one syllable.

This	is	a	hai-	ku		
I	hope	So-	phie	will	like	it
I	wrote	it	for	her		

This is Felix's haiku as it really reads.

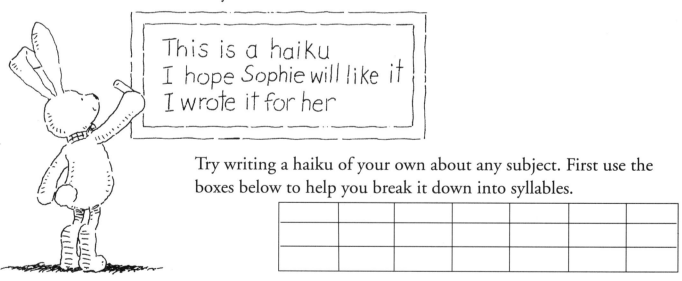

This is a haiku
I hope Sophie will like it
I wrote it for her

Try writing a haiku of your own about any subject. First use the boxes below to help you break it down into syllables.

Now write it normally without dividing it into syllables.

What's Your Favorite?

The art of printing was practiced in Japan centuries before being introduced in Europe. Making books then took much more time than it does today.

Felix is at a library and has just picked up a copy of *The Tale of Peter Rabbit.* He has snuggled up in a cozy chair to read his favorite book.

What are your favorite books? Write them here.
Then write why you like them.

1. _____

   I like it because _____

2. _____

   I like it because _____

3. _____

   I like it because _____

★★★

Eye of the Storms

A **typhoon** is a windy tropical storm that happens near Japan. In 1281, a typhoon saved Japan by preventing a foreign army from invading.

Below is a list of types of storms. Think of a place in the world where each type of storm could happen, and write it on the line. In most cases, there is more than one correct answer.

WHERE IN THE WORLD DOES IT HAPPEN?

1. Typhoon   in the Pacific Ocean near Japan _____

2. Cyclone   _____

3. Hurricane   _____

4. Monsoon   _____

5. Tornado (twister) _____

6. Blizzard   _____

solution on page 278

Puppet Show

Sophie was reading a book about Japan's history and learned about a popular type of puppet show called Bunraku. The puppets in Bunraku are as large as people. During performances, they almost seem alive. However, there are no pictures in Sophie's book, so she does not know what these puppets look like. Draw what you think they look like during a puppet show.

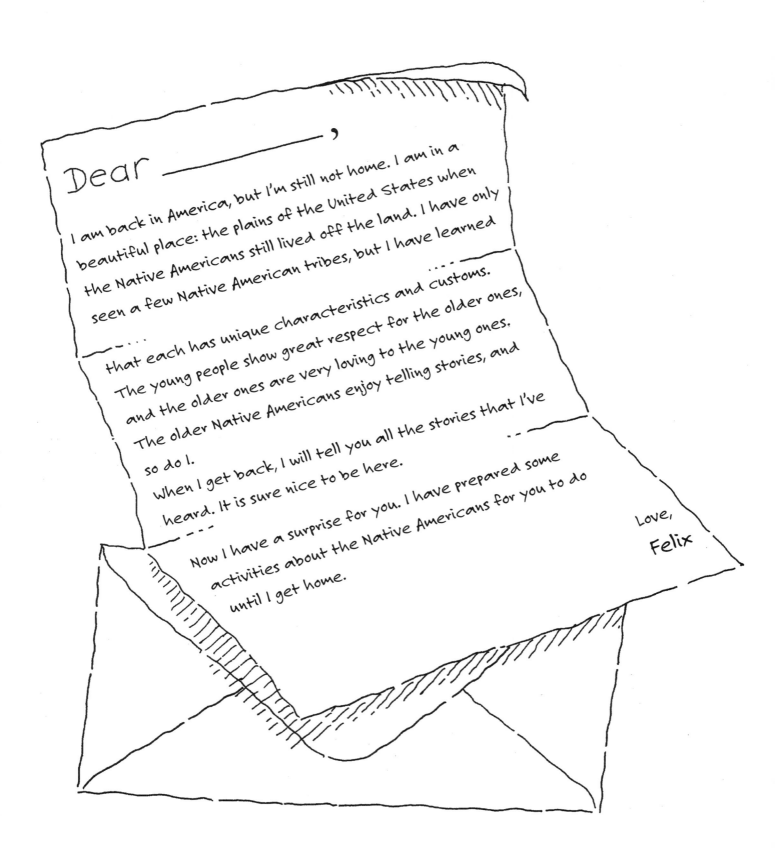

Dear _____,

I am back in America, but I'm still not home. I am in a beautiful place: the plains of the United States when the Native Americans still lived off the land. I have only seen a few Native American tribes, but I have learned

that each has unique characteristics and customs. The young people show great respect for the older ones, and the older ones are very loving to the young ones. The older Native Americans enjoy telling stories, and so do I.

When I get back, I will tell you all the stories that I've heard. It is sure nice to be here.

Now I have a surprise for you. I have prepared some activities about the Native Americans for you to do until I get home.

Love,
Felix

THE TIME OF THE NATIVE AMERICANS ON THE FRONTIER FACTS

1650 C.E.

Dates:	circa 1600–circa 1890
How the era got its name:	The frontier was the western part of North America. It later became the United States. The Native Americans lived there for many years before the Europeans arrived.
Location:	United States of America
Some important advances or inventions:	• Many names of American states, cities, and rivers such as Connecticut, Milwaukee, and the Potomac River come from Native American words
Associated people:	• Pocahontas (circa 1595–1617), Native American woman who saved the life of Captain John Smith • Sitting Bull (1834–1890), Sioux leader • Geronimo (1829–1909), Apache chief
Symbols:	• tepees • totem poles • buffalo hunting • feathers in headbands

The Name of the Game

Some Native Americans named their children after something in nature. If an infant loved taking a bath, for example, he might be named "Happy Fish." Or if a child had very bright eyes, he might be called, appropriately, "Bright Eyes."

What Native American name would you give yourself? Pick a word from Group 1 and a word from Group 2 to form an appropriate name. One example is "Running Fox."

Bright Eyes

GROUP 1	GROUP 2
Smiling	Heart
Strong	Eagle
Running	Spirit
Helpful	Wind
Clever	Rabbit
Fast	Mountain
Curious	Star
Traveling	River
Blue	Fox

Running Fox

What name did you choose and why?

_____

Now make up another Native American name using your own words.

_____

What do you think the name that your parents gave you means?

_____

Thanksgiving, 1621

This is a cartoon strip showing the beginning of a conversation between a Pilgrim and a Native American. The Pilgrims were the people who came from England and settled in Massachusetts. They held the first Thanksgiving in 1621, and they invited the Native Americans to eat with them.

Only the first panel of the cartoon has been completed. Fill in the rest of the panels with words and pictures to finish the story.

We are planning to have a feast to celebrate our harvest. Would you like to join us?

What Happened?

Read the following fictional story. A **fictional** story is one that is made up. This story is told in the **third person**. This means that the story is told by someone who doesn't take part in it. Sometimes the person who tells a story in the third person wasn't even there when it happened.

Two young Native Americans wanted to help their tribe. The chief told them that they could collect sticks to use to build tepees. One of the young men, Impatient One, did not want to do that. His friend, Mischief Finder, suggested that they hunt for food instead. The chief told them that they had enough food and did not like to waste any, so they should gather sticks. On the plains, they spotted a lone buffalo separate from its herd. Then they saw a member of their tribe whom they both admired, Great Hunter. They thought that he would kill the buffalo for their tribe. Mischief Finder shouted at the buffalo so that it would run in Great Hunter's direction, and he could hit it with his arrow. But when Great Hunter did not take out his bow and arrow, Impatient One quickly threw his spear and killed the buffalo. Both young men shouted triumphantly as Great Hunter came to them. Great Hunter scolded them for killing the buffalo, because the tribe needed other things more than that buffalo. Impatient One asked him why he was named Great Hunter. Great Hunter said that he would tell them later after they told the chief what they had done.

Impatient One   Mischief Finder   Chief   Great Hunter

Each of the four characters in the story has a different opinion about what happened. Pretend that you are each of the characters, and write the story the way you think that character sees it. Write in the boxes on the next page or use another sheet of paper if you need more room. This is called writing in the **first person**, which means that you use the word "I" often. Everyone talks in the first person. If your name were John, you would not say, "John likes reading." You would say, "I like reading." There are no right or wrong answers.

Tell the story as **Impatient One** sees it.	Tell the story as **Mischief Finder** sees it.

Tell the story as **the Chief** sees it.	Tell the story as **Great Hunter** sees it.

Through the Woods

A Native American boy wants to visit a friend in a neighboring tribe that lives across the woods, but he can't remember how to get there. Help him find his way through the forest to visit his friend by drawing a line to show his path through the maze. There is one correct answer.

START

END

solution on
page 279

Peaceful Land

Many Native Americans were surprised when foreigners began to arrive in North America. The Native Americans believed that the land belonged to everyone, so they were confused when strangers from France, Spain, and England began to buy and sell the land. The land was important to the Native American way of life, so they respected it.

Look at this picture. Sophie, Felix, and a Native American are looking at the prairie night sky. What do you think they see in the stars?

solution on page 279

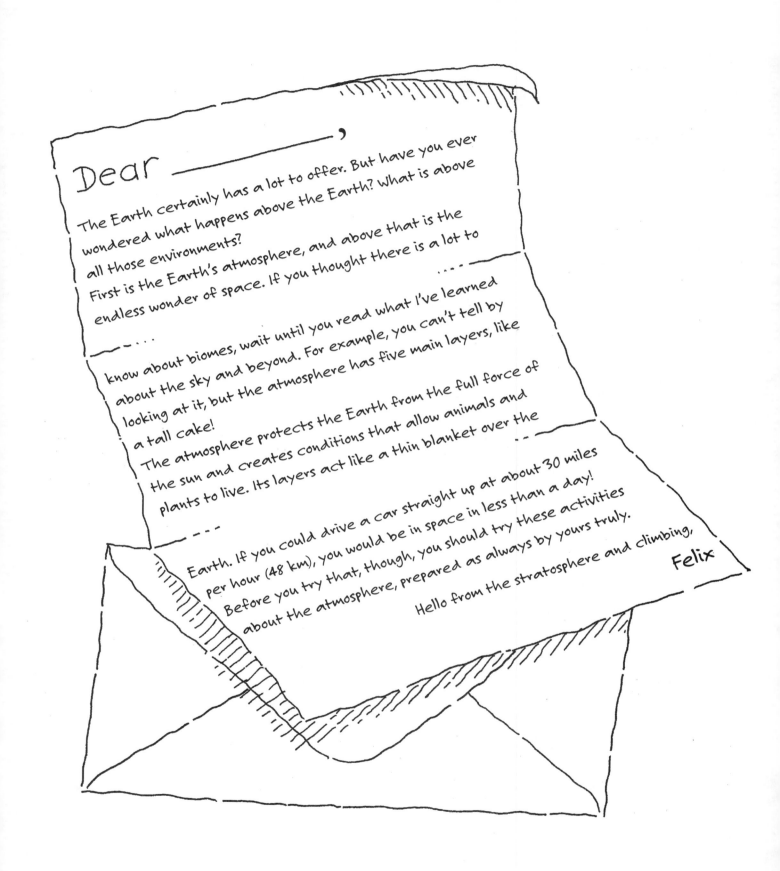

Dear _____,

The Earth certainly has a lot to offer. But have you ever wondered what happens above the Earth? What is above all those environments?

First is the Earth's atmosphere, and above that is the endless wonder of space. If you thought there is a lot to

. . . .

know about biomes, wait until you read what I've learned about the sky and beyond. For example, you can't tell by looking at it, but the atmosphere has five main layers, like a tall cake!

The atmosphere protects the Earth from the full force of the sun and creates conditions that allow animals and plants to live. Its layers act like a thin blanket over the

- -

Earth. If you could drive a car straight up at about 30 miles per hour (48 km), you would be in space in less than a day! Before you try that, though, you should try these activities about the atmosphere, prepared as always by yours truly.

Hello from the stratosphere and climbing,

Felix

Atmosphere Facts

Height of Earth's atmosphere: 620 miles (1,000 kilometers)

Number of basic atmosphere layers: 5

Combination layer: ionosphere—layer that reflects radio waves and overlaps with mesosphere and thermosphere

Atmosphere contents:
- 78 percent nitrogen
- 21 percent oxygen
- 0.9 percent argon
- 0.03 percent carbon dioxide
- traces of hydrogen, neon, helium, krypton, xenon, methane, ozone, carbon monoxide

LAYER	HEIGHT ABOVE GROUND	DESCRIPTION	DOES TEMPERATURE INCREASE OR DECREASE WITH ALTITUDE (HEIGHT)?
troposphere	0-11 miles (18 kilometers)	weather happens here	decrease
stratosphere	11-30 miles (18-50 kilometers)	average of -58°F (-50°C); contains ozone layer; most planes fly here	increase
mesosphere	30-50 miles (50-80 kilometers)	-148°F (-100°C) at top	decrease
thermosphere	50-250 miles (80-400 kilometers)	3,632°F (2,000°C) at top	increase
exosphere	250-40,000 miles (400-64,000 kilometers)	air is very thin and gas molecules are constantly "exiting" into space	does not apply

★
Where in the Air Are You?

Fill in the correct layer or layers in the box next to the statement. One is done already.

1. You are in the layer where humans live.	troposphere
2. You are in the hottest layer of the atmosphere.	
3. You are in an airplane.	
4. You see a cloud fly by.	
5. You are in the layer where it is so close to space that there is no temperature.	
6. You are in one of the layers that is warmer at the bottom	

solution on page 280

Blue Sky, White Clouds

What color is light? It seems clear, or white, doesn't it? Actually, seven colors—red, orange, yellow, green, blue, indigo, and violet—blend together to make light. This color series is called the **spectrum**.

When the sun's light enters the atmosphere, it is scattered by tiny particles of dust. Each color travels through the air like a wave. Blue wavelengths are the shortest and the easiest to scatter. That's why the sky looks blue. Red wavelengths are the longest. That's why some sunsets are red.

There are three basic types of clouds:

CLOUD		MEANING	HOW IT LOOKS	USUAL FORECAST
	cirrus	feathery	wavy, thin	clear weather will end
	cumulus	heaped	puffy, white	hot, dry
	stratus	layered	gray, covers the sky	drizzle or light snow

Draw a picture of the sun's light entering Earth's atmosphere as the full spectrum, then hitting dust and making the sky blue. Throw in a few clouds, too. There is no right or wrong answer—just use your imagination.

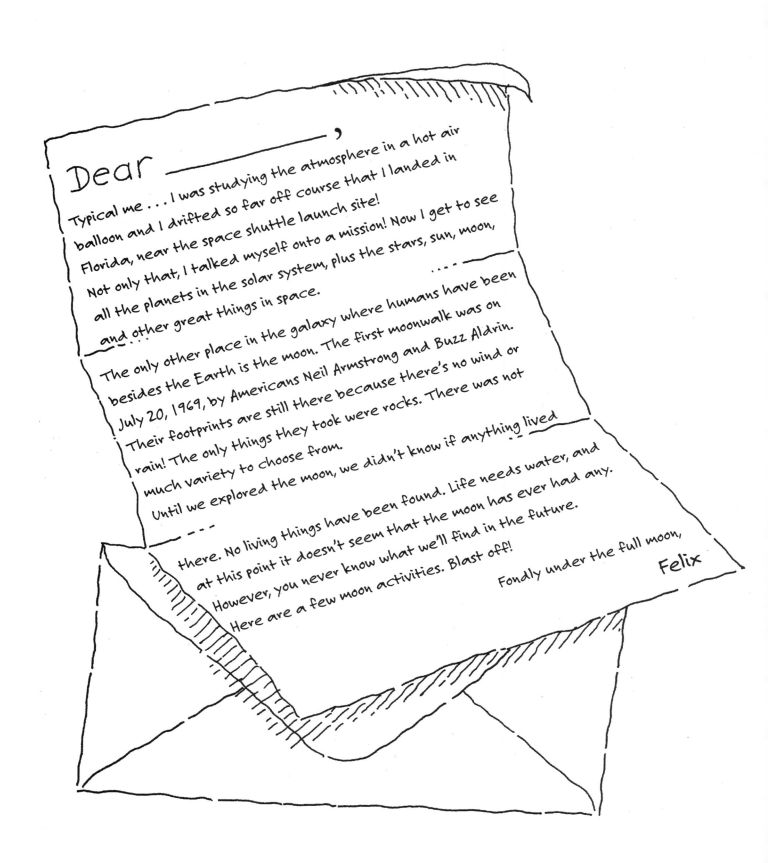

Dear _____,

Typical me . . . I was studying the atmosphere in a hot air balloon and I drifted so far off course that I landed in Florida, near the space shuttle launch site! Not only that, I talked myself onto a mission! Now I get to see all the planets in the solar system, plus the stars, sun, moon, and other great things in space.

The only other place in the galaxy where humans have been besides the Earth is the moon. The first moonwalk was on July 20, 1969, by Americans Neil Armstrong and Buzz Aldrin. Their footprints are still there because there's no wind or rain! The only things they took were rocks. There was not much variety to choose from.

Until we explored the moon, we didn't know if anything lived there. No living things have been found. Life needs water, and at this point it doesn't seem that the moon has ever had any. However, you never know what we'll find in the future. Here are a few moon activities. Blast off!

Fondly under the full moon,
Felix

Earth's Moon Facts

Another term for "moon": satellite

Number of natural satellites the Earth has: 1 (the moon)

First time an Earth craft visited the moon: 1959

Distance from Earth: 238,900 miles (384,390 kilometers), on average

Diameter: 2,160 miles (3,475 kilometers)—¼ the size of Earth

Temperature: 280°F to -148°F (138°C to -100°C)

Age: 4.6 billion years old

Atmosphere: none

Made of: rock containing elements such as aluminum, calcium, iron, and magnesium

Gravity: one-sixth of Earth's

How long it takes for the moon to revolve around the Earth: 29.5 days

Number of astronauts who have walked on the moon: 12

Size of moon compared to the United States: its diameter would almost stretch from Cleveland, OH, to San Francisco, CA

Moon adjective: lunar

Phases of the moon:
1. new—can't see the moon
2. waxing crescent—can see the curved edge of full-circle moon
3. first quarter—can see half-circle moon
4. waxing gibbous—"waxing" means "growing"
5. full—can see full-circle moon
6. waning gibbous—"waning" means "shrinking"
7. last quarter—can see half-circle moon
8. waning crescent—can see the curved edge of full-circle moon

★★★

The Moon's Revenge

The moon has no oceans, but it has a very big influence on Earth's oceans. A **tide** is the rise or fall of ocean water at the shore. Tides are caused primarily by the moon's movement around the Earth.

Low tide is when water at the shore seems to be sucked back into the ocean. **High tide** is when the water creeps a lot further onto the shore. High tide can be dangerous because water at your ankles might soon rise to your waist, or even over your head.

You need a partner and a clock with a second hand to play this game. (Do you remember what a second hand is? If not, go to page 39.) Ask someone such as a friend, sibling, or parent to do it with you.

You want to build a sandcastle on this beach near the water, but the high tide is coming in three minutes!

Look at the clock. When the second hand is at the 12, begin drawing your sandcastle on the left side of the page. Your partner will also begin drawing the high tide coming in from the right side! Every thirty seconds, your partner must draw a little more water coming closer to your sandcastle. This means your partner will get to add water six times before high time reaches the left side of the page—and your sandcastle. When the second hand hits the 12 for the third time, your three minutes are up and your partner must say "Stop!"

Everybody Line Up

Something amazing happens when the Earth, moon, and sun are positioned in a straight line. It's called an eclipse.

A **solar eclipse** is when the moon passes between the Earth and the sun, blocking the sun's brightness. The moon's shadow then covers a small part of the Earth. A long time ago solar eclipses often frightened people. They thought a monster was eating the sun!

Solar Eclipse

A **lunar eclipse** is when the Earth passes between the moon and the sun, casting a shadow on the moon so we can't see it anymore. Lunar eclipses are more common than solar eclipses. Also, they can last all night, while solar eclipses last only a few minutes.

Lunar Eclipse

Answer these eclipse questions.

1. Which is shorter, a lunar eclipse or a solar eclipse? ——————————

2. Which eclipse is visible during the day? ——————————

3. What type of eclipse can be seen more often, a lunar or a solar? ——————————

4. Which eclipse is visible at night? ——————————

5. Can lunar eclipses and solar eclipses happen at the same time? ——————————

BONUS:

6. What would you call an eclipse where Sophie stands between Felix and the sun, casting a shadow on Felix?

——————————————————

solution on page 280

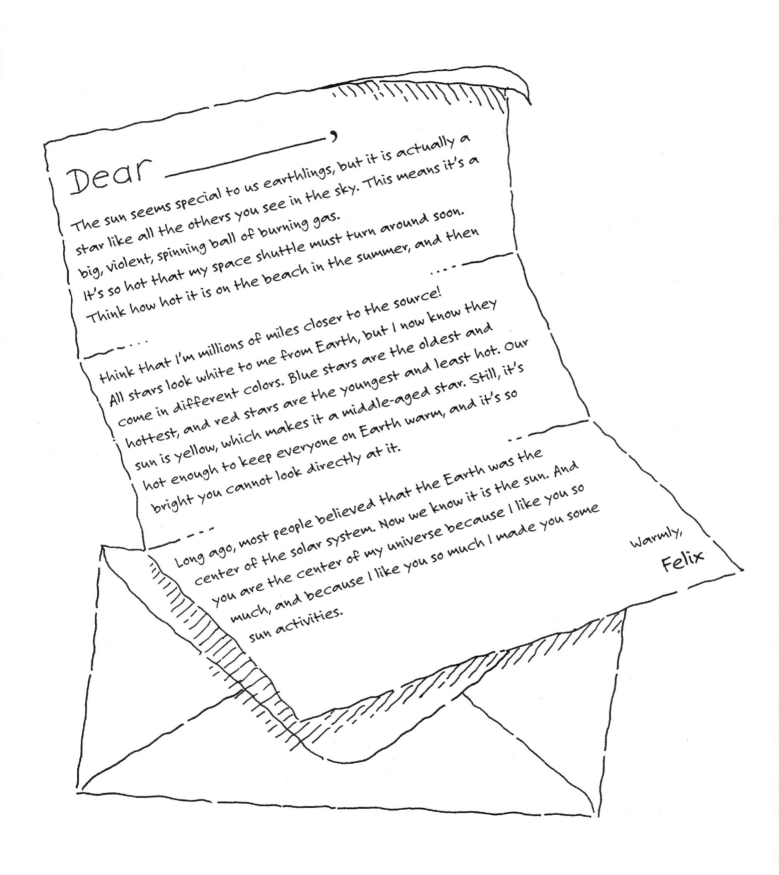

Dear _____,

The sun seems special to us earthlings, but it is actually a star like all the others you see in the sky. This means it's a big, violent, spinning ball of burning gas.

It's so hot that my space shuttle must turn around soon. Think how hot it is on the beach in the summer, and then think that I'm millions of miles closer to the source!

All stars look white to me from Earth, but I now know they come in different colors. Blue stars are the oldest and hottest, and red stars are the youngest and least hot. Our sun is yellow, which makes it a middle-aged star. Still, it's hot enough to keep everyone on Earth warm, and it's so bright you cannot look directly at it.

Long ago, most people believed that the Earth was the center of the solar system. Now we know it is the sun. And you are the center of my universe because I like you so much, and because I like you so much I made you some sun activities.

Warmly,
Felix

Sun Facts

Distance from Earth: 93 million miles (150 million km)

Diameter: 865,000 miles (1,391,785 km)—109 times the diameter of Earth

Center temperature: 25,000,000°F (14,000,000°C)

Surface temperature: 10,800°F (6,000°C)

Age: 5,000 million years

Made of: hydrogen with some helium and smaller amounts of other elements

How long it takes for the Earth to revolve around the sun: 365 or 366 days

How long it would take to drive to the sun, if that were possible: 177 years at 60 miles per hour (97 km/hr) with no stops

How long it takes light from the sun to reach Earth: 8 minutes

Number of Earths that would fit inside the sun: 1 million

Name of the surface we see: photosphere

Sun adjective: solar

Planets in the solar system, in order, from the closest to the sun to the farthest away:

1. Mercury
2. Venus
3. Earth
4. Mars
5. Jupiter
6. Saturn
7. Uranus
8. Neptune
9. Pluto
10. ? (Planet X)

Plan Ahead

The sun will die one day, but even your great-great-great-great-great-great-great-great-great-great-great-great-great-great-great-great grandkids won't have to worry about it.

In about five billion years the sun will burn up all of its hydrogen and will become a red giant star. Next it will expand so much it will probably grow past the Earth. Then it will shrink down to a white dwarf star, which will be about the size of Earth. Finally, thousands of millions of years after that, it will cool off and become what is called a black dwarf.

What do you think life will be like so far in the future? Will anything we know today still be around? Write a short story about the people—or creatures—that live on Earth five billion years in the future. Use another sheet of paper if you need more room.

_____

_____

_____

_____

_____

_____

_____

_____

_____

_____

_____

Sunshine on My Shoulder

The sun's heat allows life to exist on Earth. The sun is even warming us at night in the winter, just not as strongly as in summer. The next time you are outside on a cold, dark, winter night, look at the sky and say, "Thank you sun!" Its energy is everywhere.

Circle everything in the picture whose name includes the word sun.

solution on page 281

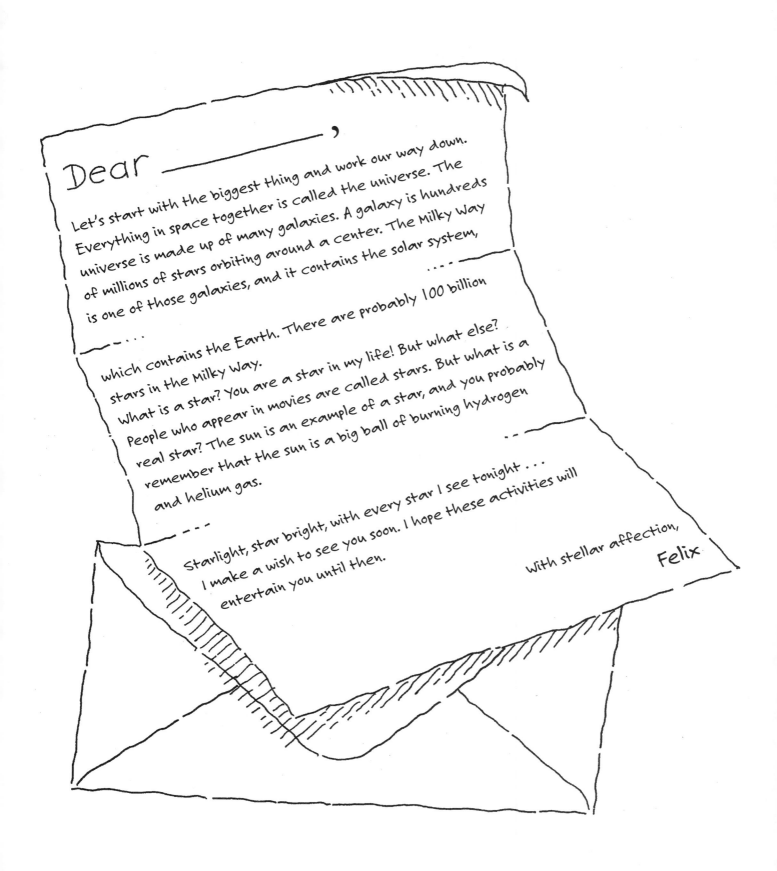

Dear _____,

Let's start with the biggest thing and work our way down. Everything in space together is called the universe. The universe is made up of many galaxies. A galaxy is hundreds of millions of stars orbiting around a center. The Milky Way is one of those galaxies, and it contains the solar system, which contains the Earth. There are probably 100 billion stars in the Milky Way.

What is a star? You are a star in my life! But what else? People who appear in movies are called stars. But what is a real star? The sun is an example of a star, and you probably remember that the sun is a big ball of burning hydrogen and helium gas.

Starlight, star bright, with every star I see tonight . . . I make a wish to see you soon. I hope these activities will entertain you until then.

With stellar affection,
Felix

Star and Galaxy Facts

*Number of galaxies
in the universe:*   100,000 million

*Number of stars in
the Milky Way
galaxy:*   100 billion

*Where our
solar system is in
the Milky Way:*   in the Orion arm, one of the four spiraling arms

*Nearest galaxy
to the Milky Way:*   Andromeda, the farthest object in space we can see in the night sky
without a telescope

Terms:
- binary star — two stars that stay together, orbiting the same center of gravity
- black hole — dark area in space whose gravity is so strong that it pulls in
everything nearby, including light; caused when a heavy star dies
- celestial — describes things in the sky or space
- constellations — eighty-eight groups of stars named for mythological beings, animals,
and objects
- nebula — bright or dark cloud of interstellar gas

- North Star,
or Polaris — current star that marks the north pole of the heavens, which is
determined by drawing an imaginary line from Earth's North Pole
into space
- nova — when a star becomes brighter for only a few weeks or years
- parallax — apparent change of a star's position due to Earth's rotation, used to
determine how far away a star is
- pulsar — celestial object, probably a type of star, that gives off radio waves
- quasars — brightest, oldest, and most distant galaxies
- supernova — explosion of a very large star
- white dwarf — small, dense remains of a dead star

Non-Dairy Galaxies

Galaxies come in three basic shapes:

1. **spiral**—these galaxies have curvy "arms" of stars circling around a disk-shaped center
2. **elliptical**—these galaxies are circular or oval, and flattened or spherical
3. **irregular**—each of these galaxies has a different formation

Most galaxies are spiral. Irregular galaxies are rare.

Ours, the Milky Way, is a spiral with four curvy arms like a pinwheel. It is called the Milky Way because it looks like a river of milk in the night sky.

Felix discovered a few new galaxies on his trip, and he wants you to name them. Write the name for each galaxy on the line next to it. There are no right or wrong answers. Then draw your own galaxy in any shape you like, and name that one, too.

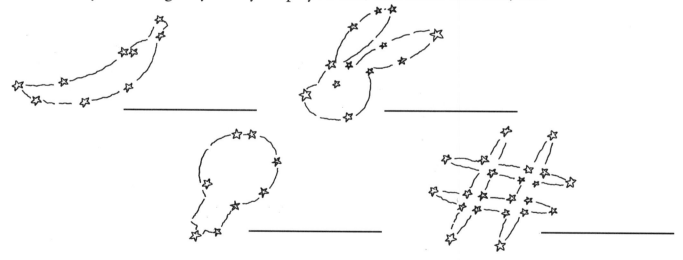

★★

Things that Go Twinkle in the Night

On many clear nights you can see special groups of stars, and you won't even need a telescope.

Thousands of years ago, astronomers wanted an easy way to remember the location of stars, so they drew imaginary pictures around them. These star pictures were then named after mythological beings, animals, or other objects and are called **constellations**. Some constellations were named in honor of someone or something even if they don't look like that person or object.

The stars in a constellation are unrelated, and they are actually very far away from one another. They are in the same constellation only because it makes a better picture.

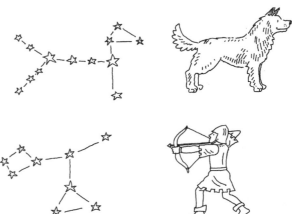

Today, the world shares eighty-eight constellations, twelve of which make up the zodiac.

These are the names of twenty constellations.

CONSTELLATION	MEANING	ALPHABETIZED	ZODIAC SIGN?
Canis Major	Big Dog		
Tucana	Toucan		
Telescopium	Telescope		
Monoceros	Unicorn		
Lacerta	Lizard		
Scutum	Shield		
Gemini	Twins		
Sagittarius	Archer		
Musca	Fly		
Cassiopeia	Queen of Ethiopia		
Cetus	Whale		
Pisces	Fish		
Hercules	Hercules		
Sagitta	Arrow		
Vulpecula	Little Fox		
Scorpius	Scorpion		
Microscopium	Microscope		
Phoenix	Phoenix		
Pictor	Painter		
Pavo	Peacock		

solution on page 281

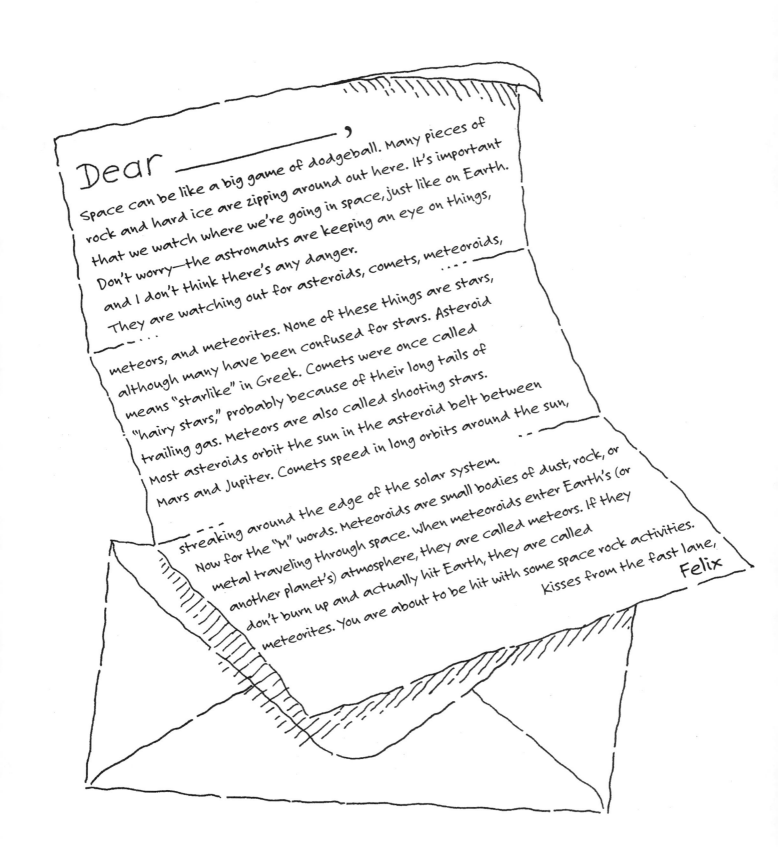

Dear _____,

Space can be like a big game of dodgeball. Many pieces of rock and hard ice are zipping around out here. It's important that we watch where we're going in space, just like on Earth. Don't worry—the astronauts are keeping an eye on things, and I don't think there's any danger. They are watching out for asteroids, comets, meteoroids, meteors, and meteorites. None of these things are stars, although many have been confused for stars. Asteroid means "starlike" in Greek. Comets were once called "hairy stars," probably because of their long tails of trailing gas. Meteors are also called shooting stars. Most asteroids orbit the sun in the asteroid belt between Mars and Jupiter. Comets speed in long orbits around the sun, streaking around the edge of the solar system.

Now for the "M" words. Meteoroids are small bodies of dust, rock, or metal traveling through space. When meteoroids enter Earth's (or another planet's) atmosphere, they are called meteors. If they don't burn up and actually hit Earth, they are called meteorites. You are about to be hit with some space rock activities.

Kisses from the fast lane,

Felix

Asteroid, Comet, Meteoroid, Meteor, and Meteorite Facts

Another term for asteroids: minor planets

Asteroids are made of: rock, some with iron and nickel

Number of asteroids: 1 million

Number of asteroids we know something about: 13,000

Number of asteroids we know a lot about: 5,000

Biggest asteroid: Ceres, 580 miles (933 km) in diameter, discovered in 1801

Smallest asteroid: 0.6 miles (1 km) in diameter

Size of most asteroids: under 62 miles (100 km) in diameter

Comets are made of: ice and dust—often called a giant, dirty snowball

Shape of a comet's orbit around the sun: elliptical

Parts of a comet: nucleus, head (ice and dust), and gaseous tail

Direction of the comet's tail: always pointing away from the sun

Another term for meteor: shooting star, falling star

Meteorites are made of: rock, metal, or both

Meteorites come from: asteroids or comets

Size of most meteorites: fist-sized

Largest meteorite found on Earth: 66 tons (60 tonnes), in Africa

Meteor showers occur when: Earth's orbit intercepts the path of a swarm of meteoroids

Number of meteor showers a year: ten; one of them, called Perseids, is usually very visible every August

Astronomer's Journal

On New Year's Day 1801, an Italian named Father Giuseppi Piazzi (1746–1826) discovered asteroids. He named the first one Ceres, after the Roman goddess of agriculture. This was a very exciting day in science history.

Write Father Giuseppi Piazzi's journal entry for January 1, 1801, just after he first saw what would soon be named an "asteroid." Also draw his sketch of Ceres. (HINT: If you aren't sure about journals, see page 233.)

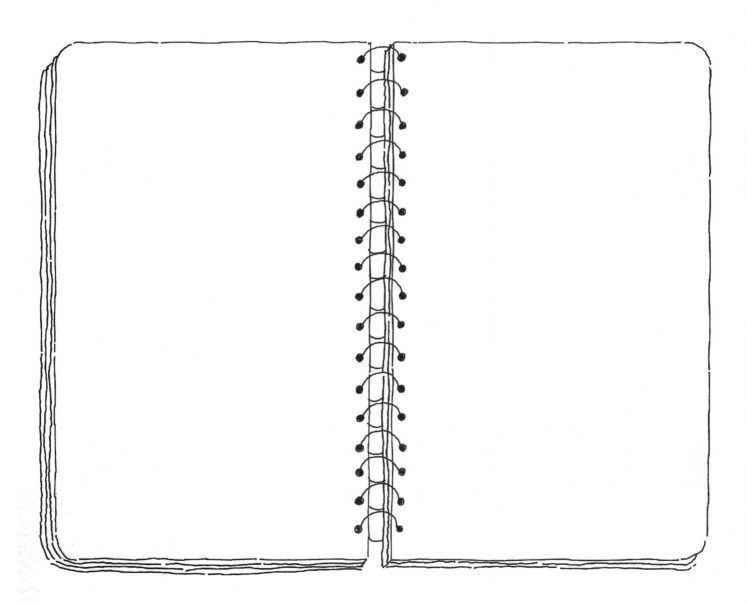

Not Your Average Meteor Shower

Felix and Sophie are watching a big meteor shower but some meteors look a bit strange.
Look closely, and circle the falling items that are not "shooting stars."

solution on page 282

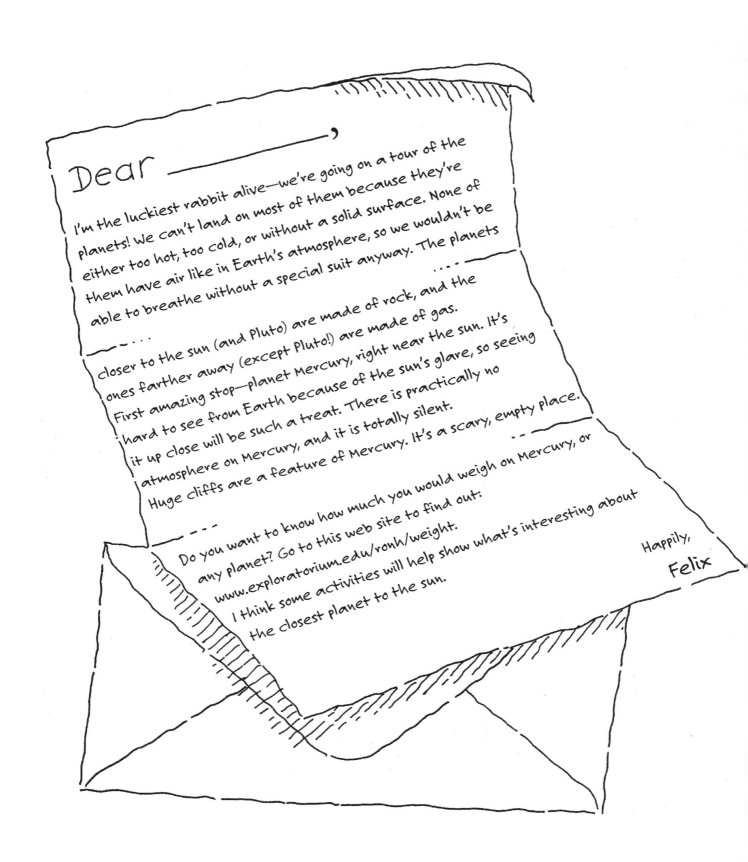

Dear ——————,

I'm the luckiest rabbit alive—we're going on a tour of the planets! We can't land on most of them because they're either too hot, too cold, or without a solid surface. None of them have air like in Earth's atmosphere, so we wouldn't be able to breathe without a special suit anyway. The planets closer to the sun (and Pluto) are made of rock, and the ones farther away (except Pluto!) are made of gas.

First amazing stop—planet Mercury, right near the sun. It's hard to see from Earth because of the sun's glare, so seeing it up close will be such a treat. There is practically no atmosphere on Mercury, and it is totally silent. Huge cliffs are a feature of Mercury. It's a scary, empty place.

Do you want to know how much you would weigh on Mercury, or any planet? Go to this web site to find out: www.exploratorium.edu/ronh/weight. I think some activities will help show what's interesting about the closest planet to the sun.

Happily,

Felix

Mercury Facts

Named after:	the Roman messenger god
Why it got that name:	it orbits the sun so quickly
Year discovered:	before 1600
First time Earth craft visited:	1973
Position from the sun:	1st planet
Distance from the sun:	36 million miles (58 million kilometers)
Diameter:	3,031 miles (4,878 kilometers)
Size compared to the other planets:	8th largest
Length of day:	59 Earth days
Length of year:	88 Earth days
Surface temperature:	-356 to 800°F (-180 to 430°C)
Atmosphere:	none
Made of:	rock with iron core
Color:	orange
Number of moons:	0
Rings:	no

★★

Name that Moon

We know Mercury has no moons, but pretend you just discovered one. Circle which of the two suggested names for the moon would fit based on its description.

EXAMPLE:

The moon is covered with water.

(Aqua) or Arid ?

Aqua is the better name. Aqua means water, and arid means dry.

1. The moon rotates very slowly.
   Tortoise or Tornado ?

2. The moon is covered with volcanoes.
   Glacier or Lava ?

3. The moon is blue.
   Cerulean or Crimson ?

4. The moon is made of rock.
   Coral or Boulder ?

5. The moon is very small.
   Miniscule or Gargantuan ?

6. You discovered the moon.
   someone else's name or your name ?

solution on page 282

★★★

Wise about Size

Of the planets, only Pluto is smaller than Mercury. If the sun were the size of a basketball, Mercury would be the size of a small seed.

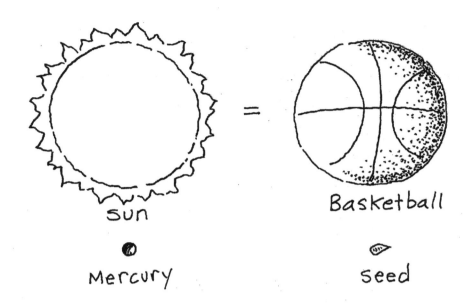

What size do you think Mercury would be if the sun were the size of each of these items? Write your answer on the lines. There are no right or wrong answers, just good guesses.

1. beach ball _____

2. bottom snowball of a snowman _____

3. hot air balloon _____

4. soccer ball _____

5. marble _____

6. big globe of the Earth like you see in museums

_____

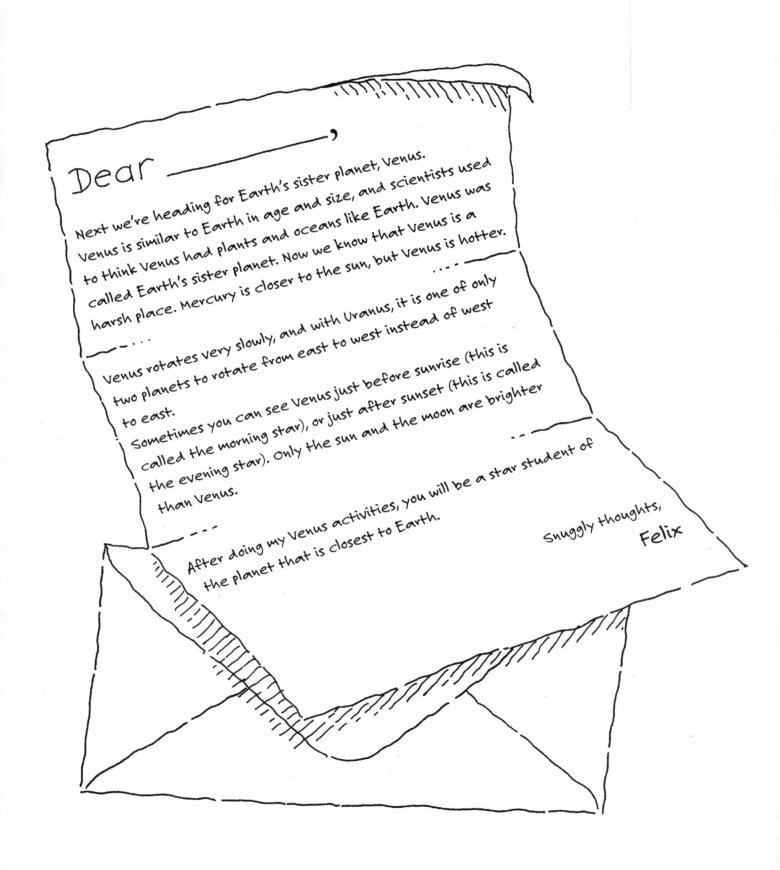

Dear _____,

Next we're heading for Earth's sister planet, Venus. Venus is similar to Earth in age and size, and scientists used to think Venus had plants and oceans like Earth. Venus was called Earth's sister planet. Now we know that Venus is a harsh place. Mercury is closer to the sun, but Venus is hotter.

- - -

Venus rotates very slowly, and with Uranus, it is one of only two planets to rotate from east to west instead of west to east.
Sometimes you can see Venus just before sunrise (this is called the morning star), or just after sunset (this is called the evening star). Only the sun and the moon are brighter than Venus.

- - -

After doing my Venus activities, you will be a star student of the planet that is closest to Earth.

Snuggly thoughts,
Felix

Venus Facts

Named after:	the Roman goddess of love and beauty
Why it got that name:	it is the brightest planet viewed from Earth
Year discovered:	before 1600
First time Earth craft visited:	1962
Position from the sun:	2nd planet
Distance from the sun:	67 million miles (108 million kilometers)
Diameter:	7,520 miles (12,102 kilometers)
Size compared to the other planets:	6th largest
Length of day:	243 Earth days
Length of year:	225 Earth days (yes, it's shorter than a Venus day!)
Surface temperature:	895°F (480°C)
Atmosphere:	carbon dioxide with thick yellow-white clouds of sulfuric acid gas
Made of:	rock with iron and nickel core
Color:	yellow
Number of moons:	0
Rings:	no

Beauty Pageant

Most features on Venus such as craters and mountains are named for female figures, and the planet has always been associated with feminine beauty.

Draw what you feel are the three
most beautiful things on Earth.
There are no right or wrong answers.

Reversed to Me Is Regular to You

On Venus, the sun rises in the west and sets in the east. Does this seem reversed?
On Earth, it's the other way around.

Circle the things in the scene that are reversed.
(HINT: There are more than five but less than ten.)

solution on
page 283

199

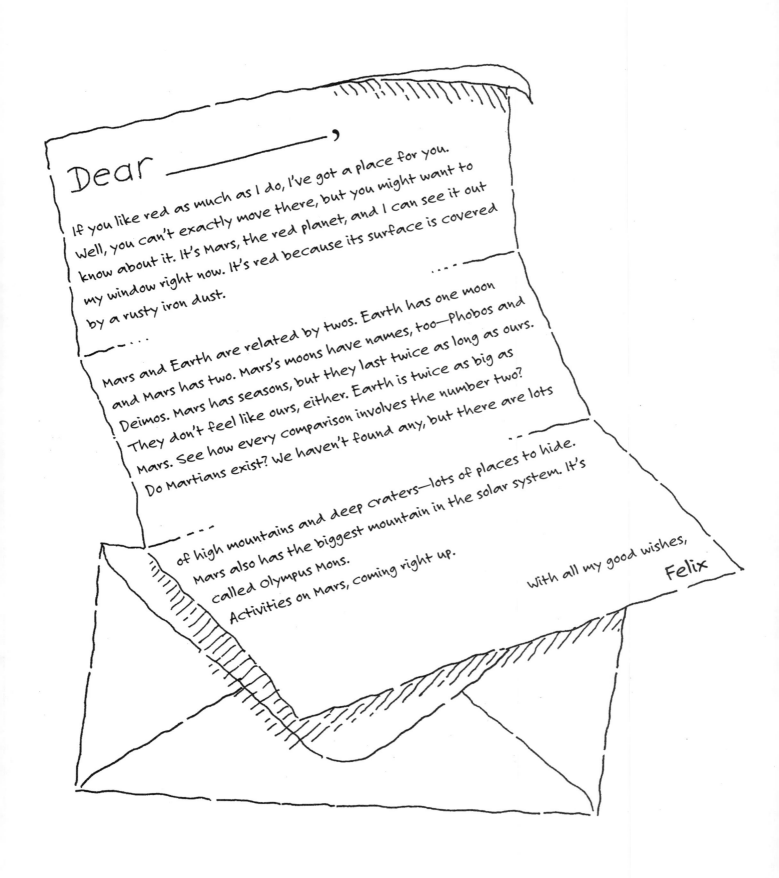

Dear _____,

If you like red as much as I do, I've got a place for you. Well, you can't exactly move there, but you might want to know about it. It's Mars, the red planet, and I can see it out my window right now. It's red because its surface is covered by a rusty iron dust.

Mars and Earth are related by twos. Earth has one moon and Mars has two. Mars's moons have names, too—Phobos and Deimos. Mars has seasons, but they last twice as long as ours. They don't feel like ours, either. Earth is twice as big as Mars. See how every comparison involves the number two? Do Martians exist? We haven't found any, but there are lots of high mountains and deep craters—lots of places to hide. Mars also has the biggest mountain in the solar system. It's called Olympus Mons.

Activities on Mars, coming right up.

With all my good wishes,
Felix

Mars Facts

Named after:	the Roman god of war
Why it got that name:	it is red like blood, which is shed in war
Year discovered:	before 1600
First time Earth craft visited:	1965
Position from the sun:	4th planet
Distance from the sun:	142 million miles (228 million kilometers)
Diameter:	4,217 miles (6,786 kilometers)
Size compared to the other planets:	7th largest
Length of day:	25 Earth hours
Length of year:	687 Earth days
Surface temperature:	-248 to 77°F (-120 to 25°C)
Atmosphere:	carbon dioxide with some nitrogen and argon
Made of:	rock
Color:	red
Number of moons:	2
Rings:	no

★★★

Mars Wordfinder

Several words are hidden in this word grid. Circle *only* the onesthat have to do with Mars. Words are either across or down.

```
M A S R O C E A N X E
T Y B A C O N M U W R
P L A N E T I A S A U
H W P I V D J K T R S
O A C M E R D Y A T T
B U R A C R E D R E Y
O P A L B D I A F I U
S E T S C O M E T R P
T S E A E I O U Y O N
M O R H W J S A I M N
V E N U S X R N S A O
O L Y M P U S M O N S
```

solution on page 283

Live from Mars, It's . . .

It's very unlikely that life ever existed on Mars, although it is a popular feature of many science fiction stories.

Mars is a cold, rocky planet with many violent dust storms. There is no liquid water, very little oxygen, and high levels of ultraviolet radiation.

Draw what you think a Martian would look like based on the severe conditions on Mars. There are no right or wrong answers.

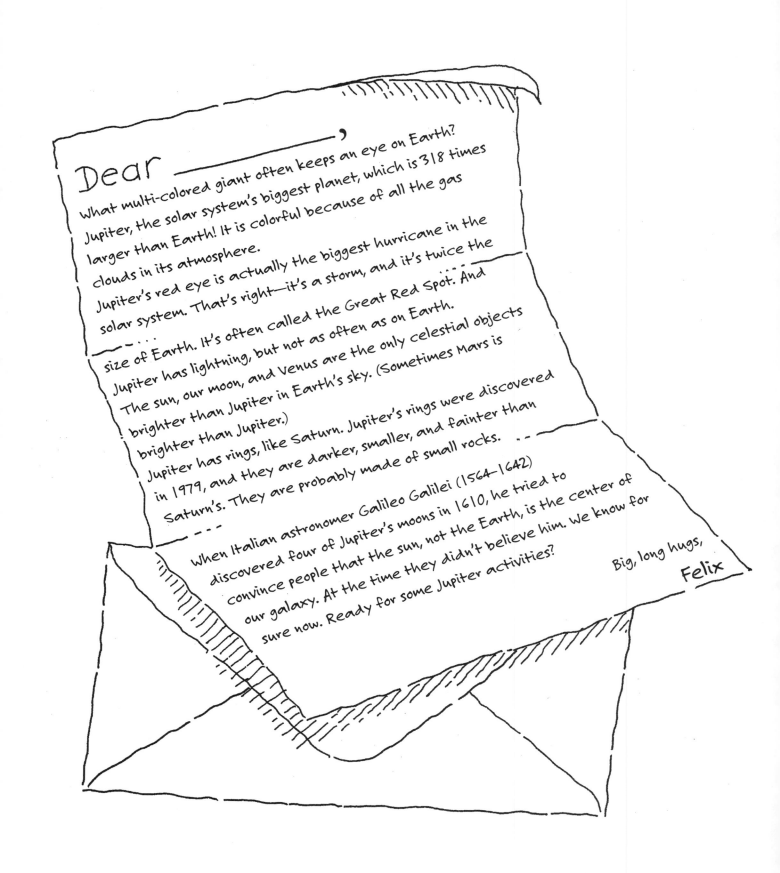

Dear _____,

What multi-colored giant often keeps an eye on Earth? Jupiter, the solar system's biggest planet, which is 318 times larger than Earth! It is colorful because of all the gas clouds in its atmosphere.

Jupiter's red eye is actually the biggest hurricane in the solar system. That's right—it's a storm, and it's twice the size of Earth. It's often called the Great Red Spot. And Jupiter has lightning, but not as often as on Earth. The sun, our moon, and Venus are the only celestial objects brighter than Jupiter in Earth's sky. (Sometimes Mars is brighter than Jupiter.)

Jupiter has rings, like Saturn. Jupiter's rings were discovered in 1979, and they are darker, smaller, and fainter than Saturn's. They are probably made of small rocks.

When Italian astronomer Galileo Galilei (1564–1642) discovered four of Jupiter's moons in 1610, he tried to convince people that the sun, not the Earth, is the center of our galaxy. At the time they didn't believe him. We know for sure now. Ready for some Jupiter activities?

Big, long hugs,

Felix

Jupiter Facts

Named after:	the Roman king of the gods
Why it got that name:	it is the biggest planet
Year discovered:	before 1600
First time Earth craft visited:	1973
Position from the sun:	5th planet
Distance from the sun:	484 million miles (778 million kilometers)
Diameter:	88,849 miles (142,984 kilometers)
Size compared to the other planets:	largest
Length of day:	10 Earth hours
Length of year:	12 Earth years
Surface temperature:	-238°F (-150°C)
Atmosphere:	hydrogen with some helium, methane, ammonia, and water vapor
Made of:	hydrogen in metallic and liquid form with small rock core
Colors:	yellow, red, brown, white
Number of moons:	16
Rings:	yes

An Intriguing Moon

Jupiter is named after the Roman king of the gods. Jupiter's moons are named for figures from his life.

The names of the four moons that Galileo discovered in 1610 are Io, Europa, Ganymede, and Callisto. They are each larger than the other twelve Jupiter moons. These moons were discovered before the planets Uranus, Neptune, and Pluto.

Europa is covered in ice but may have a liquid ocean beneath it, and that ocean may contain life.

Europa

Answer the questions. There are no right or wrong answers.

1. Do you think there is life in the universe besides on Earth?_____

2. Do you think there is life in our galaxy besides on Earth? _____

3. Do you think there is life on Europa? _____

4. If so, what kind of life do you think it is? _____

_____

Fast Planet

Jupiter spins on its axis faster than any other planet. Its day is only ten Earth hours long.

Circle the pictures of the things that move fast.

Do you think any of the things you circled move faster than Jupiter? _____

solution on page 284

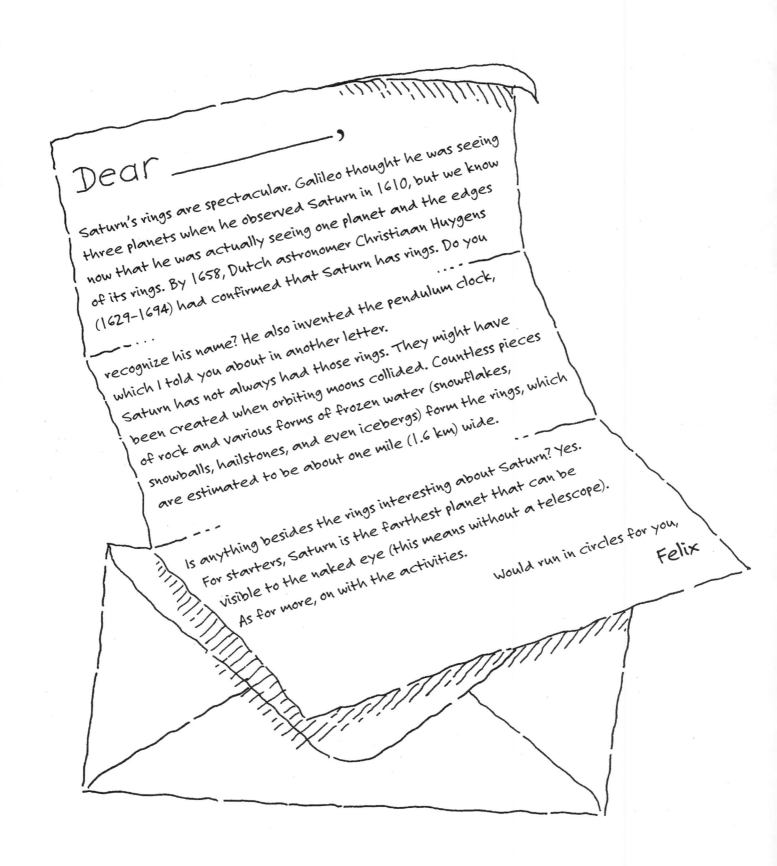

Dear _____,

Saturn's rings are spectacular. Galileo thought he was seeing three planets when he observed Saturn in 1610, but we know now that he was actually seeing one planet and the edges of its rings. By 1658, Dutch astronomer Christiaan Huygens (1629–1694) had confirmed that Saturn has rings. Do you recognize his name? He also invented the pendulum clock, which I told you about in another letter.

Saturn has not always had those rings. They might have been created when orbiting moons collided. Countless pieces of rock and various forms of frozen water (snowflakes, snowballs, hailstones, and even icebergs) form the rings, which are estimated to be about one mile (1.6 km) wide.

Is anything besides the rings interesting about Saturn? Yes. For starters, Saturn is the farthest planet that can be visible to the naked eye (this means without a telescope). As for more, on with the activities.

Would run in circles for you,

Felix

Saturn Facts

Named after:	the Roman god of agriculture
Why it got that name:	Saturn was the father of Jupiter
Year discovered:	before 1600
First time Earth craft visited:	1979
Position from the sun:	6th planet
Distance from the sun:	887 million miles (1,427 million kilometers)
Diameter:	74,900 miles (120,536 kilometers)
Size compared to the other planets:	2nd largest
Length of day:	10 Earth hours
Length of year:	29.5 Earth years
Surface temperature:	-292°F (-180°C)
Atmosphere:	hydrogen with some helium and methane
Made of:	hydrogen in metallic and liquid form with rock and ice core
Color:	yellow
Number of moons:	18
Rings:	yes

The Naked Eye

Although it is not as bright as Jupiter, Saturn can be seen in the night sky without a telescope. It doesn't twinkle like stars do. And to see its rings you do need a telescope.

Seeing something with a **naked eye** means you don't use any mechanical equipment. Many distant bodies in space or tiny organisms cannot be seen without a telescope or microscope.

Draw an eye next to any object that can be seen with the naked eye.

clover

Saturn

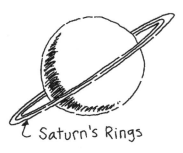

Blue Whale

Earth's Moon

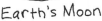

Saturn's Rings

Amoeba

Asteroid Belt

solution on page 284

Everybody out of the Pool

If we could put Saturn in a gigantic body of water, it would float! It's the only planet whose density is less than water's.

Building a tank or pool big enough to hold Saturn, the solar system's second biggest planet, would be impossible. Pretend it isn't, and fill in the rest of the panels of this cartoon strip with words and pictures to finish the story.

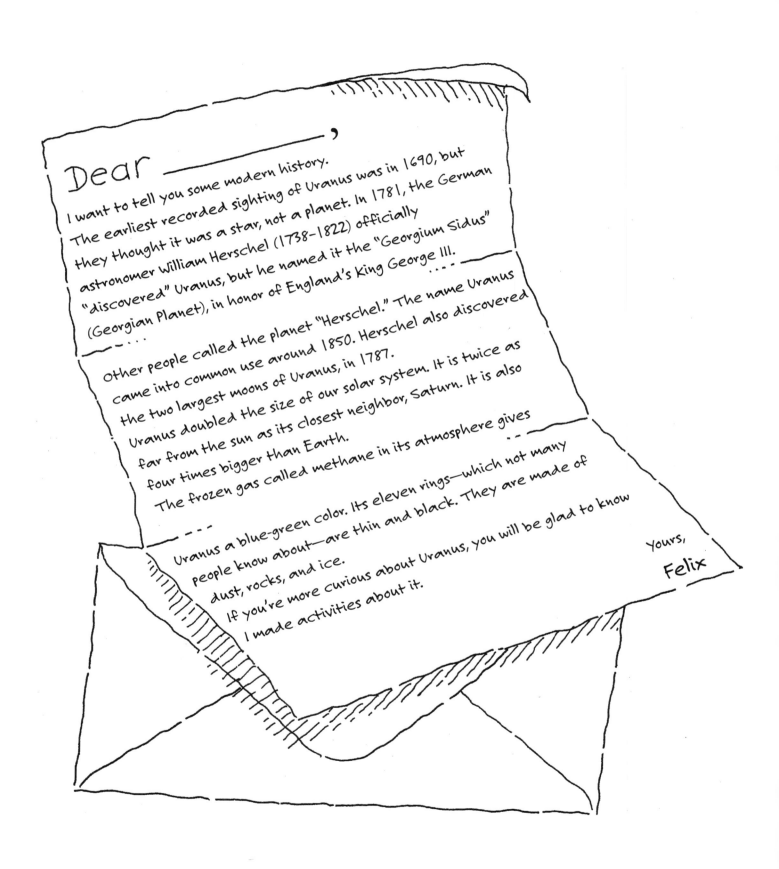

Dear _____,

I want to tell you some modern history. The earliest recorded sighting of Uranus was in 1690, but they thought it was a star, not a planet. In 1781, the German astronomer William Herschel (1738–1822) officially "discovered" Uranus, but he named it the "Georgium Sidus" (Georgian Planet), in honor of England's King George III.

Other people called the planet "Herschel." The name Uranus came into common use around 1850. Herschel also discovered the two largest moons of Uranus, in 1787.

Uranus doubled the size of our solar system. It is twice as far from the sun as its closest neighbor, Saturn. It is also four times bigger than Earth.

The frozen gas called methane in its atmosphere gives Uranus a blue-green color. Its eleven rings—which not many people know about—are thin and black. They are made of dust, rocks, and ice.

If you're more curious about Uranus, you will be glad to know I made activities about it.

Yours,
Felix

Uranus Facts

Named after: the Roman god of the heavens

*Why it got
that name:*   Uranus was the father of Saturn

Year discovered: 1781 (March 13)

*First time
Earth craft visited:*   1986

*Position from
the sun:*   7th planet

*Distance from
the sun:*   1,782 million miles (2,870 million kilometers)

Diameter: 31,764 miles (51,118 kilometers)

*Size compared to
the other planets:*   3rd largest

Length of day: 17 Earth hours

Length of year: 84 Earth years

Surface temperature: -353°F (-214°C)

Atmosphere: hydrogen, helium, and methane

Made of: water, ice, ammonia, and methane with rock core

Color: green

Number of moons: 15

Rings: yes

Tipping Permitted

Uranus is sideways! At some point in the past, it might have been hit by large object that tipped it over. Uranus is the only planet that is sideways.

Since a year on Uranus equals eighty-four years on Earth, this means that Uranus's North Pole faces the sun for forty-two years (which is only half a year on Uranus!), then its South

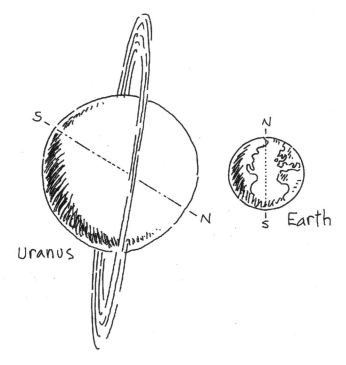

Read these statements. Put a check in the first column if the statements apply only to Uranus, and put a check in the second empty column if they apply to Uranus and other planets, too. One is done already.

STATEMENT	URANUS ONLY	URANUS AND OTHER PLANETS
I am sideways.	✔	
I have rings.		
I have moons.		
I have fifteen moons.		
I am named for a Roman god.		
I was discovered in 1781.		

solution on page 284

Marvelous Moon Math

Uranus has fifteen moons. Some were discovered from Earth. We didn't know about the rest until 1986, when a spacecraft named Voyager 2 sent back photographs of more Uranus moons as it flew by the planet.

How many of Uranus's fifteen moons were discovered on Earth? Answer these Uranus questions and do the math to find out.

QUESTION	ANSWER
How many Earth hours equal one day on Uranus?	
What day in March 1781 was Uranus discovered?	
Which Voyager spacecraft took pictures of Uranus?	
How many planets are closer to the sun than Uranus?	
How many rings does Uranus have?	
How many planets are bigger than Uranus?	
How many Uranus moons did Herschel discover?	

Rewrite the answers in the same order and calculate:

_____ - _____ + _____ + _____ - _____ + _____ + _____ = ☐

The answer is the number of Uranus's moons that were discovered on Earth.

solution on page 285

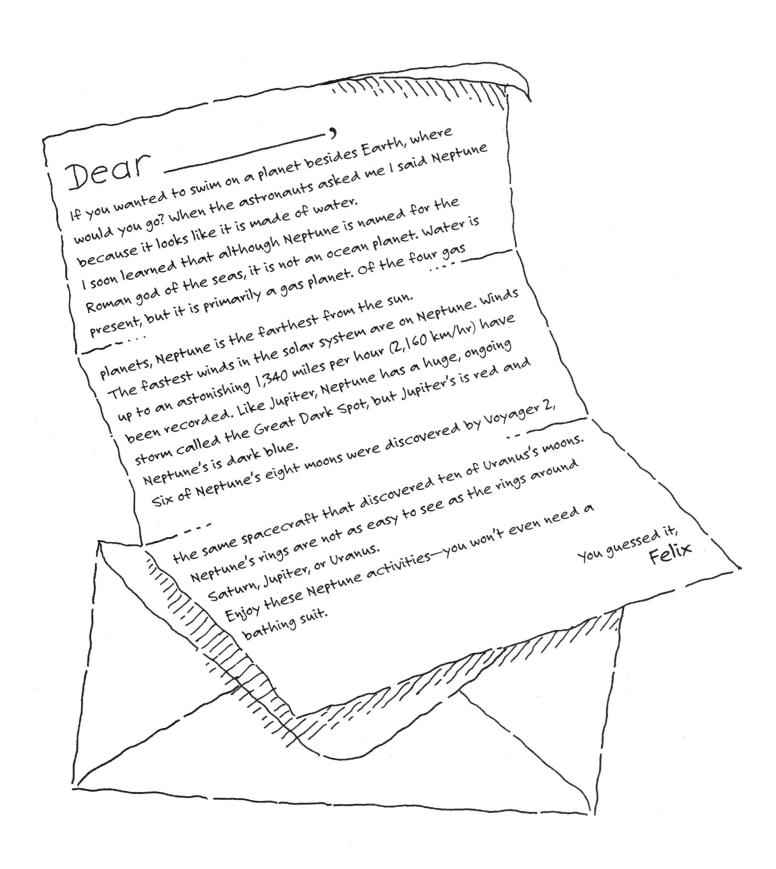

Dear _____,

If you wanted to swim on a planet besides Earth, where would you go? When the astronauts asked me I said Neptune because it looks like it is made of water.

I soon learned that although Neptune is named for the Roman god of the seas, it is not an ocean planet. Water is present, but it is primarily a gas planet. Of the four gas planets, Neptune is the farthest from the sun.

The fastest winds in the solar system are on Neptune. Winds up to an astonishing 1,340 miles per hour (2,160 km/hr) have been recorded. Like Jupiter, Neptune has a huge, ongoing storm called the Great Dark Spot, but Jupiter's is red and Neptune's is dark blue.

Six of Neptune's eight moons were discovered by Voyager 2, the same spacecraft that discovered ten of Uranus's moons. Neptune's rings are not as easy to see as the rings around Saturn, Jupiter, or Uranus.

Enjoy these Neptune activities—you won't even need a bathing suit.

You guessed it,
Felix

Neptune Facts

Named after:	the Roman god of the seas
Why it got that name:	it is blue like seawater
Year discovered:	1846 (September 23)
First time Earth craft visited:	1989
Position from the sun:	usually the 8th planet, sometimes the 9th, depending on where Pluto is
Distance from the sun:	2,774 million miles (4,497 million kilometers)
Diameter:	30,757 miles (49,528 kilometers)
Size compared to the other planets:	4th largest
Length of day:	16 Earth hours
Length of year:	165 Earth years
Surface temperature:	-364°F (-220°C)
Atmosphere:	hydrogen, helium, and methane
Made of:	methane, ammonia, water, and ice with rock core
Color:	blue
Number of moons:	8
Rings:	yes

★★

Stormy Trio

Neptune has three storms that don't go away.

The Great Dark Spot is a storm that rotates around the southern part of Neptune. It is as big as Earth. The Small Dark Spot is the second storm. It is about the size of Earth's moon. The third storm is a mysterious white cloud that seems to follow the other storms around. Its name is more playful—Scooter.

Write tonight's weather report for Neptune. Someone who reports and forecasts Earth's weather is called a **meteorologist**. Try to make the weather seem exciting.

_____

_____

_____

_____

_____

_____

_____

_____

Neptune's Gentlemen

Two men from different countries each predicted the existence of Neptune in 1845. They didn't know each other. They didn't even know about each other.

The Englishman, John Couch Adams (1819–1892), was a self-taught astronomer who shared his theory with the British government. The Frenchman, Urbain Jean Joseph Leverrier (1811–1877), was also an astronomer, and he was the one who named Neptune and originally got credit for discovering it.

However, scientists in England and France argued over which of their men deserved the credit. Adams and Leverrier didn't want to argue. They had become good friends, and seemed happy just to know that they helped.

In the end, it was actually German astronomer Johann Gottfried Galle (1812–1910) who used the ideas of Adams and Leverrier to find Neptune in the sky.

Answer the questions.
There are no right or wrong answers.

1. You and your best friend find ten dollars, and the police say you may keep it. How would you split the money? _____
   _____

2. You and your best friend work together on a school project, and you both do the same amount of work. Whose name goes first on the project? _____
   _____

3. You and your best friend are throwing a baseball around. He throws to you, but you miss it, and the ball breaks a school window. Who is responsible? _____
   _____

4. You and your best friend discover a new planet! Who do you name the planet after?

   _____
   _____

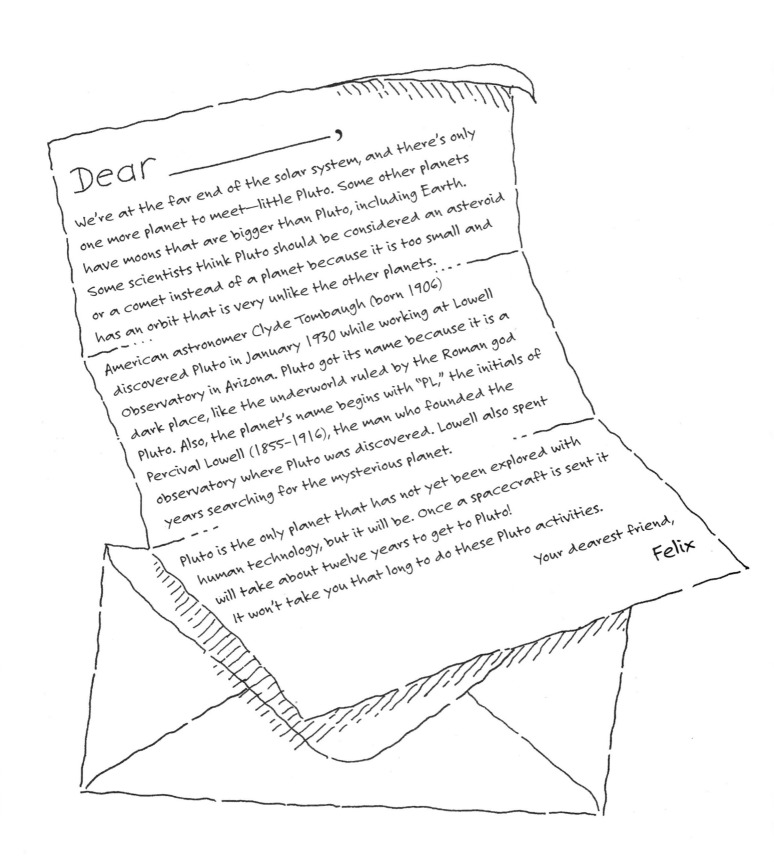

Dear _____,

We're at the far end of the solar system, and there's only one more planet to meet—little Pluto. Some other planets have moons that are bigger than Pluto, including Earth. Some scientists think Pluto should be considered an asteroid or a comet instead of a planet because it is too small and has an orbit that is very unlike the other planets.

American astronomer Clyde Tombaugh (born 1906) discovered Pluto in January 1930 while working at Lowell Observatory in Arizona. Pluto got its name because it is a dark place, like the underworld ruled by the Roman god Pluto. Also, the planet's name begins with "PL," the initials of Percival Lowell (1855–1916), the man who founded the observatory where Pluto was discovered. Lowell also spent years searching for the mysterious planet.

Pluto is the only planet that has not yet been explored with human technology, but it will be. Once a spacecraft is sent it will take about twelve years to get to Pluto! It won't take you that long to do these Pluto activities.

Your dearest friend,
Felix

Pluto Facts

Named after:	the Roman god of the underworld
Why it got that name:	it is so far from the sun that it is always dark
Year discovered:	1930 (February 18)
First time Earth craft visited:	not yet!
Position from the sun:	usually the 9th planet, sometimes the 8th, depending on where Neptune is
Distance from the sun:	3,672 million miles (5,913 million kilometers)
Diameter:	1,419 miles (2,284 kilometers)
Size compared to the other planets:	9th largest
Length of day:	6 Earth days
Length of year:	248 Earth years
Surface temperature:	-382°F (-230°C)
Atmosphere:	nitrogen, methane, and carbon monoxide
Made of:	ice, water, and methane with rock core
Color:	yellow
Number of moons:	1
Rings:	no

★★

The Big Switcheroo

Cutting in line is rude. Everyone knows that. Except Pluto.

Pluto is considered the ninth planet in our solar system. However, it has a very unusual orbit that crosses Neptune's orbit at times. When this happens, Neptune becomes the ninth planet from the sun, and Pluto becomes the eighth. In fact, Pluto was closer to the sun than Neptune from 1979 until 1999.

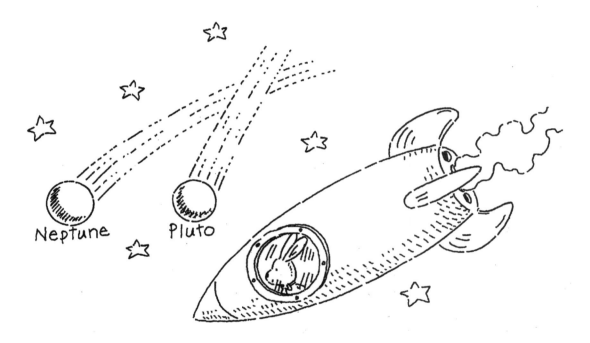

In each of these lists, one item has cut in line. Circle it. One is done already.

1. Sunday, Monday, Friday, Tuesday, Wednesday, Thursday, Saturday

2. a, b, c, d, e, f, g, h, i, j, k, l, n, m, o, p, q, r, s, t, u, v, w, x, y, z

3. June, July, August, September, November, October

4. 1998, 1997, 1999, 2000, 2001, 2002

5. nursery school, kindergarten, 2nd grade, 1st grade, 3rd grade

6. millimeter, centimeter, kilometer, meter

solution on page 285

Planet X Marks the Spot

Pluto is not the most recent planet to be discovered. In the 1990s, several other planets were found, but they were not in our solar system. Pluto is the most recent planet to be found in our solar system.

However, some scientists think a tenth planet may exist beyond Pluto. They call it Planet X. If it exists, it may be too far away for current telescopes to see.

This is a simple map of the solar system. The only objects shown are the edge of the sun and a few dots to represent the asteroid belt. Draw in the nine planets and their moons if you want. Remember which planets are big and which are small. If you think there is a Planet X, add an "X" to your map where you think it is.

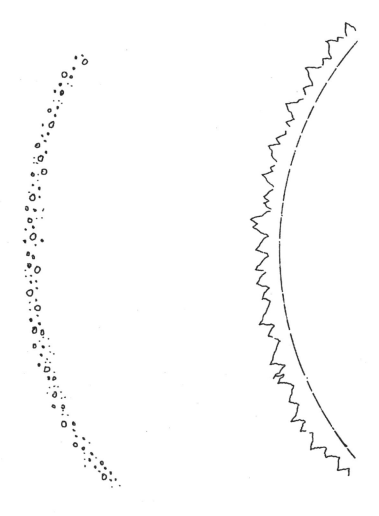

RABBIT RERUN

Dear _____,

All good things must come to an end . . .

. . . but not yet.

To do these last activities, you might have to retrace the steps of our journey from the beginning.

Love,
Felix

Living in the Past

Some of our friends in history have also gotten lost, like Felix. Luckily, they can count on someone who knows all about the past—you—to help them! Help our friends get home by drawing a line from each person to his or her house.

In which house would you best like to live and why? _____

In which house would you least like to live and why? _____

solution on page 286

Hidden in Paris

This is a picture of a busy street in Paris. By accident, Felix dropped a toy from each of the other five places that he visited. Each toy is a replica of a famous building or symbol from each of the places. A **replica** is a copy of something, often smaller than the actual thing.

Find the items that are out of place and write where Felix got them below. You must find them all—they're for Sophie!

THE TOY	WHERE FELIX GOT IT
1. _____	_____
2. _____	_____
3. _____	_____
4. _____	_____
5. _____	_____

solution on page 286

★★

Color the World

The world has seven continents. A **continent** is a large land area on the earth.
Color each continent, then write the name of the continent and the color you used
in the spaces provided below.

	CONTINENT NAME	COLOR
1.		
2.		
3.		
4.		
5.		
6.		
7.		

solution on page 286

Then and Now

People change with the times, but there are some things that they always need, such as food and clothing. Most things people used in the past still exist today but in a modern form.

Draw a line between the items used by people from the past (in the **THEN** column) and their newer versions (in the **NOW** column). Remember, you are trying to match things that have similar purposes. On the lines, write what each of the pairs has in common. One is done already.

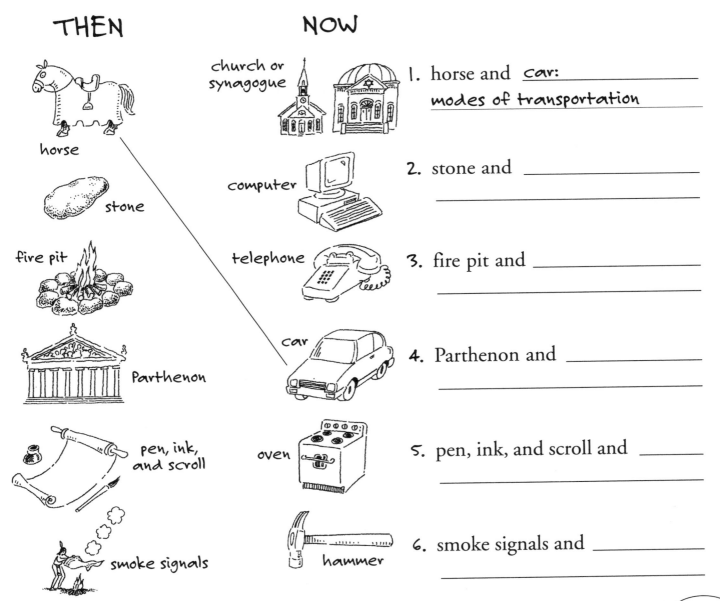

THEN

horse

stone

fire pit

Parthenon

pen, ink, and scroll

smoke signals

NOW

church or synagogue

computer

telephone

car

oven

hammer

1. horse and _car:_ _modes of transportation_

2. stone and _____ _____

3. fire pit and _____ _____

4. Parthenon and _____ _____

5. pen, ink, and scroll and _____ _____

6. smoke signals and _____ _____

solution on page 286

★★

Lay It on the Line

Think of the most special things that have happened to you in your life. Here are some possibilities:

- The day you were born
- Your first day of school
- The day you moved

- The day you met your best friend
- The day you got your favorite toy or book
- The day your brother or sister was born

Draw or write the events that are important to you. Label each event with the year that it happened or how old you were when it happened. Next, draw or write the events in the order in which they took place along the line below. This is called a **time line**. You can see an example of a time line at the beginning of the "History" section on pages 120 and 121.

Write your birthday below

_____

MONTH   DAY   YEAR

The day
you were born

World According to Felix

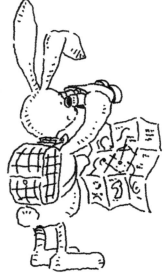

1. By visiting London, Paris, Rome, Cairo, Nairobi, and New York City, Felix sets foot on how many continents?

_____

2. Name the four continents that Felix didn't see on that trip.

_____

3. Which of the cities that Felix visits are the capitals of their countries?

_____

This is a **Mercator projection**, a kind of map on which the entire globe is flattened out so you can see it all at once. You have just discovered a new piece of land somewhere on the map. Draw it in and name it. Then draw a dot showing the location of its capital city and name that, too. Maybe Felix can visit your new country next!

solution on page 287

★★

Journal

A **journal** is a book in which you can write about what happens in your life every day. In a journal, you can write all the foods you eat in a day, the television shows you watch, the games you play, the places you visit, or the people you see. You can write your thoughts about anything at all, even private thoughts. All you need to start a journal is a blank pad of paper, a pencil or pen, and your imagination. At the end of each day, write the date and then anything you want about what happened to you that day. As the days go by, you will see how much you have done and learned. It will be fun to go back and read what you wrote.

Use this page to try writing a journal entry.

Today's date _____

_____

_____

_____

_____

_____

_____

_____

_____

_____

_____

_____

_____

Capitals Quiz

Six capital cities are listed below. Draw lines to match each city with its country and with the picture that is associated with that capital.

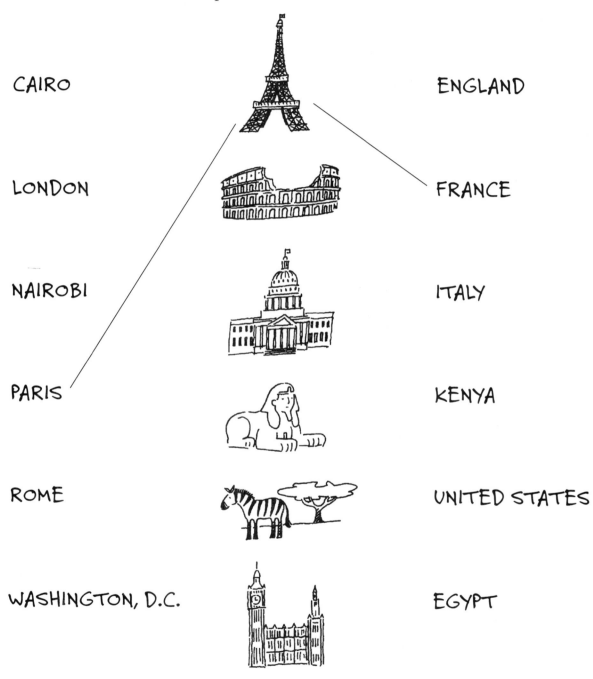

CAIRO   ENGLAND

LONDON   FRANCE

NAIROBI   ITALY

PARIS   KENYA

ROME   UNITED STATES

WASHINGTON, D.C.   EGYPT

solution on page 287

★★★

Over Yonder

Felix visited six cities: London, England; Paris, France; Rome, Italy; Cairo, Egypt; Nairobi, Kenya; and New York City, United States.

Answer the following questions about these cities, all of which have to do with distance.

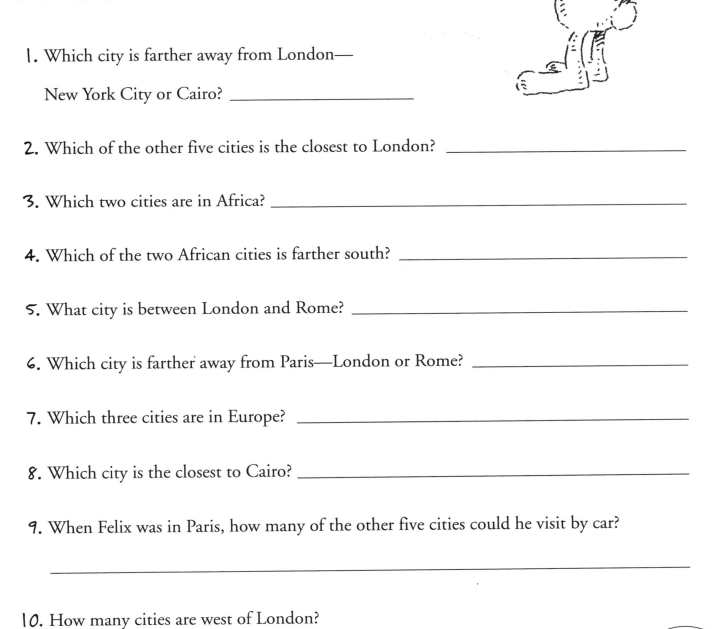

1. Which city is farther away from London—

   New York City or Cairo? _____

2. Which of the other five cities is the closest to London? _____

3. Which two cities are in Africa? _____

4. Which of the two African cities is farther south? _____

5. What city is between London and Rome? _____

6. Which city is farther away from Paris—London or Rome? _____

7. Which three cities are in Europe? _____

8. Which city is the closest to Cairo? _____

9. When Felix was in Paris, how many of the other five cities could he visit by car?

   _____

10. How many cities are west of London?

solution on page 287

_____

Stamp It!

Every country has its own postage stamps, and no matter what you are interested in, you can find stamps to match those interests. History, science, sports, art, music, animals, and many other subjects have all been pictured on stamps.

Color these six stamps that Felix got for you in New York City. In the blank space, create your very own stamp!

★★

The ABCs of Letter Writing

Long before telephones were invented, the main way people communicated over long distances was by writing letters. People wrote letters just to say hello or to describe their lives and adventures. Imagine that you are on a trip and you want to write to your friends and family. Write a letter that describes your adventure. Remember, your family knows nothing about the foreign land you have traveled to, so tell them everything!

Dear —————,

Branching Out

Draw ten ornaments on this Christmas tree, one for each country in which Felix learned about Christmas. Use an object from each country's Christmas celebration. For example, you could draw a box in honor of England's Boxing Day.

★★

Holiday Shuffle

Felix knows a few holidays are coming up, but he's a long way from a calendar. He thinks one might be Halloween, and another might be Thanksgiving. He gets a mysterious letter that tells him he's wrong, but that he can find out the correct holidays by following each step.

HALLOWEEN	WORD AFTER CHANGE IS MADE
Change the "LL" to an "N."	
Change the "EE" to an "A."	
Change the "O" to the vowel that comes after "O."	
Change the "H" to a "K."	
Change the second "N" to an "H."	
Move the "K" to where the "W" is, and remove the "W."	
Put a "CH" back in front.	

This is the holiday ⤴

THANKSGIVING	WORD AFTER CHANGE IS MADE
Take out all the "G"s.	
Take out all the "I"s.	
There is 1 vowel left. Add 2 more of the same at the end.	
Change the "T" to a "C."	
Change the "H" to a "W."	
Replace the "SVN" with a "Z."	
Move the "K" to where the "C" is, and remove the "C."	

This is the holiday ⤴

solution on page 288

Connecting the Celebrations

Draw a line between the holiday on the left and a symbol associated with that holiday on the right.

crown of
evergreen leaves

Christmas in China

white horse

dreidel

Kwanzaa

Christmas in Mexico

paper lantern

Christmas in Sweden

kinara

Chanukah

Christmas in the Netherlands

piñata

solution on
page 288

240

Make Time for Fun

Fill in these schedules. One is for an average school day, the other is for whichever holiday you celebrate—Christmas, or the first day of Chanukah, or the first day of Kwanzaa. If you don't celebrate any of these holidays, write a schedule for any holiday you choose.
There are no right or wrong answers.

AVERAGE SCHOOL DAY		HOLIDAY (write yours):	
Time of day	What I will do	Time of day	What I will do
7:00 A.M.		7:00 A.M.	
8:00 A.M.		8:00 A.M.	
9:00 A.M.		9:00 A.M.	
10:00 A.M.		10:00 A.M.	
11:00 A.M.		11:00 A.M.	
12:00 P.M.		12:00 P.M.	
1:00 P.M.		1:00 P.M.	
2:00 P.M.		2:00 P.M.	
3:00 P.M.		3:00 P.M.	
4:00 P.M.		4:00 P.M.	
5:00 P.M.		5:00 P.M.	
6:00 P.M.		6:00 P.M.	
7:00 P.M.		7:00 P.M.	
8:00 P.M.		8:00 P.M.	
9:00 P.M.		9:00 P.M.	

Do you like one of these two days better than the other? _____

If so, why? _____

If not, why not? _____

★★

All I Want for Christmas Is a Biome

Two biomes are listed after all the countries where Felix celebrated Christmas, but only one of the biomes can be found in that country. Circle the correct biome.

1. England — **desert** or **temperate forest?**

2. Sweden — **temperate forest** or **polar tundra?**

3. The Netherlands — **temperate forest** or **grasslands?**

4. Germany — **tropical rain forest** or **temperate forest?**

5. Italy — **taiga** or **mountain?**

6. Russia — **taiga** or **ocean?**

7. China — **desert** or **polar tundra?**

8. Australia — **taiga** or **desert?**

9. Mexico — **ocean** or **desert?**

10. United States — **mountain** or **taiga?**

Polar Tundra   taiga

solution on page 289

Call Me a Rat, Snake, or Pig—I Don't Mind

In the Chinese calendar every year is named in honor of an animal.

Buddhism is a religion that is practiced in China. It was founded in India by a man named Buddha (566?-480? B.C.E.). Once, Buddha asked all animals to visit him, but only twelve showed up. He rewarded those animals by naming a year after each of them, in the order that they came.

What are the twelve animals? Read each description to figure out what type of animal it is. Write your guess in the ANIMAL column. There is only one right answer for each.

DESCRIPTION	ANIMAL	YEARS
Looks like a bigger, uglier mouse		1948, 1960, 1972, 1984, 1996
Large bull with big horns		1949, 1961, 1973, 1985, 1997
Orange-and-black striped wild cat		1950, 1962, 1974, 1986, 1998
Felix!		1951, 1963, 1975, 1987, 1999
Fictional, fire-breathing lizard		1952, 1964, 1976, 1988, 2000
Slithering reptile with no legs		1953, 1965, 1977, 1989, 2001
Every cowboy and cowgirl rode one		1954, 1966, 1978, 1990, 2002
White, woolly farm animal, says "baa"		1955, 1967, 1979, 1991, 2003
Small, chattering ape with tail		1956, 1968, 1980, 1992, 2004
Male chicken, says "cock-a-doodle-doo"		1957, 1969, 1981, 1993, 2005
Common pet, "man's best friend"		1958, 1970, 1982, 1994, 2006
Pudgy, pink farm animal, says "oink"		1959, 1971, 1983, 1995, 2007

Special personality traits are associated with each animal. The Chinese believe that the year you were born has great influence on your life.

solution on page 289

Your Dark Side

What do sundials and eclipses have in common? They both create shadows.

When the sun is low in the sky, your shadow is much longer than you are. When the sun is high, your shadow is shorter than you are. When the sun is directly overhead, you only have a small shadow between your feet.

Here Felix is walking through the desert at three different times of day. Draw his shadow for each time.

solution on page 290

How to Un-Endanger Species

In the late 1970s, the peregrine falcon was the first animal on the endangered species list. An **endangered species** is an animal or plant that may die out if its home is not protected. Living things may become endangered or even extinct because of predators, a low reproduction rate, disease, and the destruction of their habitats by humans.

Some extinct animals are the dodo (a bird), great auk (a bird that looks like a penguin), passenger pigeon, Tasmanian wolf, tarpan (a type of wild horse), and Balinese tiger.

Some animals that are endangered are the mountain gorilla, giant panda, tiger, snow leopard, whooping crane, black rhino, California condor, and wild yak.

Make a list of your own called "How to Un-Endanger Species," and suggest ways to help animals and plants that are threatened. If you fill the lines and have more suggestions, write them underneath. There are no right or wrong answers.

Earth Day, Every Day—and Everywhere?

The first Earth Day was April 22, 1970. Earth Day is not Earth's birthday, but it is a very special day. It reminds us of the importance of keeping our planet clean. Cutting down on air pollution, saving endangered species, and keeping litter off our streets are all situations that might be discussed on Earth Day.

Pretend you are organizing special days for the other planets. Earth Day encourages us to be good to our environment. Write what each of those days would encourage. There are no right or wrong answers.

NAME OF SPECIAL DAY	WHAT THIS DAY ENCOURAGES
Mercury Day	
Venus Day	
Mars Day	
Jupiter Day	
Saturn Day	
Uranus Day	
Neptune Day	
Pluto Day	

Chain, Chain, Chain of Food

A **food chain** is the order in which living things eat each other, or are eaten. Rabbits eat plants, and that's a food chain. Rabbits eat plants, then foxes eat rabbits, and that's a larger food chain. Many food chains exist in every ecosystem, and they join together to form a **food web.**

Another way to write this food chain: plant, rabbit, fox

plant

rabbit

fox

These are six lists of living things from food chains. Rearrange the order to form the correct food chain, using each living thing only once.

EXAMPLE:

large bird, insect, small bird: insect, small bird, large bird

1. lion, antelope, grass	
2. chicken, human, worm	
3. krill, killer whale, blue whale	
4. bear, clam, fish, plant plankton	
5. frog, snake, leaf, owl, grasshopper	
6. sparrow, tree leaves, vulture, caterpillar, eagle	

frog

snake

leaf

owl

grasshopper

Food chains involve the sun (which allows plants to grow), a plant, a **herbivore** (plant eater), and a **carnivore** (meat eater) or **omnivore** (plant and meat eater). Often they involve more than one carnivore or omnivore.

solution on page 290

Superlative Ecosystems

Polar tundras are generally considered the **harshest** of all ecosystems.

Tropical rain forests have the **most** types of animals and trees of any ecosystem.

Deserts are the **driest** ecosystem.

Mountains are made of the **most** types of other ecosystems.

Oceans are the **largest** ecosystem.

A **superlative** is a word that describes something that is the best or the most. In the sentence "The cheetah is the **fastest mammal**," the word **fastest** is a superlative.

Find the superlatives in these sentences and circle them. If the sentence does not have a superlative, write **no superlative** next to it. If the sentence has a false superlative, write **false** next to it.

1. Sophie is the smartest girl in her class._____

2. The owl is the biggest bird in the world._____

3. What do you think is the scariest movie ever made?_____

4. Felix is the most polite rabbit of them all._____

5. Everyone likes chocolate._____

6. Who has the most money?_____

solution on
page 290

Asteroids, Comets, and Meteorites, Oh My!

Read the statements and determine if the answer is asteroid, comet, meteorite, or none.
Write each answer in the box next to each statement.

1. I am made of dirty ice.	
2. I am one of many that orbit the sun in a belt.	
3. Before I landed on Earth I was called a meteor.	
4. I have a tail.	
5. My name means "starlike."	
6. I am a star.	

solution on page 291

Cosmic Disturbance

Something has gone wrong in the sky—all the planets have moved out of order! Well, this didn't really happen, but pretend it did, and draw the planets in order of size, with the biggest near the sun and smallest the farthest away.

solution on
page 291

Know Your Roots

The month March gets its name from the planet Mars. The day Monday gets its name from the moon. The day Saturday gets its name from the planet Saturn.

March 🌑 Mars						
Sun	Mon	Tues	Wed	Thurs	Fri	Sat
	🌓 1	2	3	4	5	🪐 6
7	🌓 8	9	10	11	12	🪐 13
14	🌓 15	16	17	18	19	🪐 20
21	🌑 22	23	24	25	26	🪐 27
28	🌑 29	30	31			

Answer these name questions.

1. Where does your name come from?_____

_____

2. If you are named after a person, what do you know about that person?_____

_____

3. Is there someone in your life you might like to name your child after one day?_____

_____

4. If so, why might you want to name your child after this person?_____

_____

5. If you have a pet, is he or she named after something?_____

_____

6. If so, who or what is your pet named after?_____

_____

★★

You Must Remember This

There are easy ways to help your memory. A **mnemonic** (pronounced as if the first "m" is not there) is a rhyme or sentence used to remember lists. It may seem like nonsense, but it does the trick.

To remember the names and order of the planets, try using this mnemonic:
Many very excited monkeys juggle seven uncooked noodles perfectly.
It's silly, right? And where are the planets? Look again:

Many (Mercury)

Very (Venus)

Excited (Earth)

Monkeys (Mars)

Juggle (Jupiter)

Seven (Saturn)

Uncooked (Uranus)

Noodles (Neptune)

Perfectly (Pluto)

Or the principles of Kwanzaa:

Ugly (unity)

Salamanders (self-determination)

Wiggle (work)

Eagerly (economics)

Practicing (purpose)

Crazy (creativity)

Flips (faith)

Create a mnemonic for the four time zones in America and another for the five levels of Earth's atmosphere. Write them on the lines. There are no right or wrong answers.

AMERICAN TIME ZONES (4)

_____

_____

_____

_____

LEVELS OF EARTH'S ATMOSPHERE (5)

_____

_____

_____

_____

_____

★★★

An End Is a Beginning

After each of these six celestial terms, write other space words whose names begin with their last letter. One is done already. There is no correct number of answers.

Europa	asteroid, asteroid belt, Andromeda, Armstrong (Neil)
Saturn	
Scutum	
Venus	
Neptune	
Io	

solution on page 291

SOLUTIONS

 Holidays - Christmas Solutions

Swedish and Light: Christmas in Sweden (page 13)

Items that could add light to your St. Lucia costume:

 flashlight

 bright yellow sunglasses

 glow stick

 gold bracelet

 face glitter

And the Horse He Rides In On: Christmas in the Netherlands (page 14)

1. There are hoof prints from a single animal in your yard.

   Sinterklaas (he rides a horse)

2. There are hoof prints from more than one animal in your yard.

   Santa Claus (his sled is led by eight reindeer)

3. It is December 6.

   Sinterklaas

4. You can't put your shoes on without dumping a few presents out of them first.

   Sinterklaas

5. Someone with the initials "SP" signed your parents' guest book.

   Sinterklaas (it's his helper, Swarte Piet)

6. You were very good this year.

   Sinterklaas or Santa Claus (both reward you for being good)

BONUS:

Sinterklaas is the patron saint of **children**!

Tree History: Christmas in Germany (page 15)

There is no right or wrong answer, but Felix guesses that Martin Luther cut down the unique tree. ①

Witch Holiday Is This Again? Christmas in Italy (page 16)

1. Thanksgiving, third Thursday in November
2. St. Valentine's Day, February 14
3. Independence Day, July 4
4. no holiday
5. New Year's Eve/Day, December 31–January 1
6. St. Patrick's Day, March 17
7. no holiday

BONUS:

8. Memorial Day, last Monday in May or Veterans' Day, November 11

Down Under the Tree: Christmas in Australia (page 19)

A Smashing Time: Christmas in Mexico (page 20)

There are twenty-one treats falling from the piñata. Were you close? Were you exactly right?

Comes But Once a Year: Christmas in the United States (page 21)

HOUSE 1: Sophie's family's house
HOUSE 2: home only until 6:15 P.M.—first
HOUSE 3: home only from 6:30 to 6:45 P.M.—third
HOUSE 4: home only from 6:10 to 6:30 P.M.—second
HOUSE 5: home at 6:50 P.M.—fourth
The order they should carol is house 2, then 4, then 3, then 5 . . . then home to house 1.

Holidays - Chanukah Solutions

Victory of the Few over the Many (page 24)

The underdogs are circled.

1. War—an army with 5,000 soldiers or an army with 50,000 soldiers
2. Nature—a cat or a mouse
3. Spelling bee—a student who studied a word list for two hours or a student who studied a word list for ten minutes
4. Football—a team of eleven players or a team of eight players
5. Art show—an artist whose paintings are displayed at the front of the gallery or an artist whose paintings are displayed in the back of the gallery

BONUS:

6. Football—a team of eleven inexperienced players or a team of eight experienced players

The underdog depends on what you think is more important, size or skill. In other words, either team could be the underdog. This also applies to number 4.

Spin Control (page 26)

1. Sophie plays dreidel with two friends. Each starts with ten pennies and puts one in the center. Sophie spins first, gets the **shin**, and takes the appropriate action. How many pennies are in the center now? 4
2. By the time Sophie spins next, there are five pennies in the center. She gets the **shin** again! She takes the appropriate action. How many pennies does she have now? 8
3. Later, on Sophie's last spin, there are ten pennies in the center, and she gets the **hei**. How many pennies does she take from the center? 5

BONUS:

4. Sophie's friend once played dreidel and got the **nun** every time. How many pennies did he have at the end if he started with twenty? 20

All I Need Is a Miracle (page 27)

There really are no right answers, but most people agree that a baby being born is truly a miracle—and that happens thousands of times a day all around the world!

Holidays - Kwanzaa Solutions

A Candle a Day (page 30)
The examples are rearranged so that they are next to the matching principle.

unity -------------------------coming together with family
self-determination ------------being determined to improve one of your skills
work --------------------------helping a neighbor clean his or her garage
economics ----------------------saving money to open a store with a friend some day
purpose ------------------------setting a goal to help someone in need
creativity ----------------------painting a mural on a wall at school
faith --------------------------believing in your teachers

In Search of Principles (page 31)

```
K A J U N I A O T A E
U U K B Z I E Y L V M
U M L B E O P Y A N C
M T A M U W U J I M A
B O L S M C U M O V R
A L E I O M D A E P G
H I Y R J S U L E A S
O U J M A D J F G I O
T V E O N A A I B M I
L A C R E O M P S A K
I B G O L I A O E N M
K U J I C H A G L I A
```

Original Colors (page 32)
These colors can symbolize anything they make you feel, but here are some possibilities.

Red   love, anger, fire, strength
Black   silence, night, cold, mystery
Green   envy, plants, water, coolness

Time Solutions

Time Pieces (page 38)

1. Eating a bowl of cereal usually takes about ten **minutes**.
2. When you drop a pencil, it hits the ground in one or two **seconds**.
3. A full moon is visible once a **month**.
4. Except in the summer, you probably go to school five days a **week**.
5. A century is one hundred **years**.
6. At the end of every **day**, you go to sleep.
7. Most movies are about two **hours** long.

Help Yourself to Seconds (page 39)

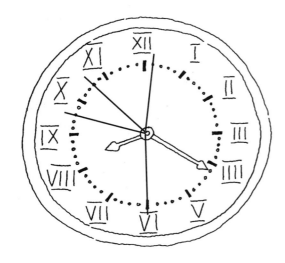

Save the Day (page 40)

The summer photograph should have a light sky, and the winter photograph should have a dark sky. The colors are up to you.

Let's Do the Time Zone Again (page 41)

1. What time zone is New York City in?   Eastern
2. What time zone is Louisiana in?   Central
3. Which time zone includes the fewest states?   Pacific
4. How many states (whole or partial) are in the Mountain time zone?   thirteen
   (Montana, North Dakota, South Dakota, Oregon, Idaho, Wyoming, Nebraska, Utah, Colorado, Kansas, Arizona, New Mexico, Texas)

The Biggest Clock (page 42)

1. You must be in school at 8 o'clock. What does your sundial look like when you arrive? 8 o'clock

2. Your mother leaves the house at 10 A.M. one Saturday for three hours. What time is it when she returns? 1 o'clock

3. At 3 o'clock you decide you want to go a store that closes at 5 o'clock and that is one hour away. What is the latest time you can leave to get there by the time it closes? 4 o'clock

4. On a camping trip you wake up in the middle of the night to get a drink of water. Your counselor says, "Go to bed. It's 3 o'clock in the morning," but you don't think it's that late. What does your sundial show? No shadow—in the middle of the night the sundial is useless. You need sunlight to read a sundial!

Find the Time (page 43)

Once upon a time, a girl named Meridiem lived in a crowded city with her father and mother. The junkyard they owned was next to their apartment building. Her father called their junkyard "a big pile of things whose time ran out."

Meridiem would wake up with enough time to have a warm breakfast before school. When she had time she would stop at a fruit stand to buy a fresh apple with some of the money her parents gave her for lunch.

"How are you today?" Meridiem asked the fruit-stand vendor.

"Tired from getting up so early," the fruit-stand vendor said. "And still I never have enough time to do what I want."

Meridiem nodded sadly and kept walking. A clock on a building showed the time to be 7:50 A.M. She had time to stop at the newsstand to look at her favorite magazine.

"Good morning," she said to the newsstand vendor.

"There was a time when every morning was good," the newsstand vendor said. "Now people don't have time to read, and I don't sell many papers."

"I'm sorry. I would buy one if I had enough money."

"Don't worry about money, Meridiem. It's time that is important. Spend it wisely."

It was almost 8:00 A.M., and if Meridiem was late for school one more time, she knew she would get in trouble. She rushed.

(continued on page 260)

Time Solutions (continued)

Find the Time (continued from page 259)

That night Meridiem thought about the two vendors. She couldn't give them more time, but she could make time nicer for them. She had an idea.

In the morning she got up extra early so she could go to the junkyard. It took her some time before she found two antique clocks that still worked. She cleaned them and found that they looked quite distinguished. Then she left for school.

First she stopped at the fruit vendor's stand and gave him one of the clocks.

"Thank you, Meridiem. I will keep this clock on my stand all day to remind me how much time I really do have."

Meridiem smiled and hurried to the newsstand, where she gave the vendor the other clock.

"What a surprise. Thank you! But I told you to spend your time wisely. Why did you get this wonderful clock for me?"

"I thought it was so handsome that people might stop and ask what time it is, and then they might buy a paper," she said. "Besides, I had a little extra time this morning."

How many times does the word ~~time~~ appear in the story? **eighteen**

Blackout (page 44)

Time Enough at Last (page 46)
The order from least amount of time
  to most:
1. spell your first name
2. eat a banana
3. watch your favorite cartoon
4. get a good night's sleep
5. drive a car from New York to Florida

London Solutions

Ahead of Time (page 54)

1. (C.) When it is 12:00 in the afternoon in London, it is 7:00 in the morning in Mansfield.
2. (B.) Felix in London goes to bed first because it gets late there first!
3. (A.) Yes it is already the new year in London when it reaches midnight on New Year's Eve in Mansfield.
4. Sophie in Mansfield would not want to call Felix in London before she goes to bed at 8:00 at night because it would be 1:00 in the morning in London! Felix would be fast asleep!
5. (A.) Yes, when Sophie goes to school in Mansfield at 9:00 in the morning, London children are still in school, because it is 2:00 in the afternoon there. Remember, London children don't get out of school until 3:00 in the afternoon.

London Jumble (page 56)

1. ENGLAND
2. QUEEN
3. BRIDGE
4. KING
5. BOBBY

BONUSES:

1. THAMES
2. UNION JACK
3. DOUBLE DECKER

License to Drive (page 57)

 United States, because it is American money

 London, because the British have a royal family

 London, because drinking tea in the late afternoon is a British custom

 United States, because it is an American sport

Paris Solutions

One Word Leads to Another (page 60)

There are many correct answers, but here are some possibilities:

	COUNTRY	CITY	TYPE OF FOOD	SCHOOL SUBJECT	BODY OF WATER
P	Portugal Poland	Paris Prague	peas pizza	physics physical education	Pacific Ocean pond
A	Argentina Australia	Athens Atlanta	apples artichokes	arithmetic anatomy	Atlantic Ocean Adriatic Sea
R	Russia Rwanda	Rome Rio de Janeiro	rice radishes	reading	river Rhine River
I	Ireland Israel	Istanbul Ithaca	ice cream	industrial arts international studies	Indian Ocean
S	South Africa Sweden	Sarajevo San Francisco	spaghetti salmon	science social studies	sea stream

The View from Here (page 61)

You should find and color the following items:

- book
- dog
- pair of eyeglasses
- baguette
- clock

Oddballs (page 62)

1. Cathedral is not a food.
2. Pizza is not a French food.
3. Wine is a drink, and the others are all food.
4. Church is the only word that does not begin with the letter "b."
5. Champs Elysées is a street, and the others are all structures.
6. Carrot is the only type of food that would not appear with the word "French" before it.
7. Paris is a city, and the others are all countries.
8. Nile is the only river that is not in France.

Speak French (page 63)

1. *Le garçon entend le vent.* (The boy hears the wind.)
2. *La fille achète un bonnet.* (The girl buys a hat.)
3. *Le garçon porte des gants et une écharpe.* (The boy wears gloves and a scarf.)
4. *La fille déblaye la neige avec une pelle.* (The girl shovels snow with a shovel.)

Can You Spare a Dollar? (page 64)

1. You would need ~~five~~ (5) French francs to buy the soda.
2. You would need ~~ten~~ (10) French francs to buy the ice cream.
3. You would need ~~thirty~~ (30) French francs to buy the book.

What's for Lunch? (page 65)

You should find and color the following items:

- baguette
- cheese
- wine

 Rome Solutions

Rome Was Built in a Day (page 68)

1. England — Rome is a city in Italy, not England.
2. Island — Rome is not an island.
3. French — People in Rome speak Italian.
4. Elevators — The Colosseum is much too old to have elevators!

Eternally Rome (page 69)

This is the code:

1 = A	2 = B	3 = C	4 = D	5 = E	6 = F	7 = G	8 = H	9 = I
10 = J	11 = K	12 = L	13 = M	14 = N	15 = O	16 = P	17 = Q	18 = R
19 = S	20 = T	21 = U	22 = V	23 = W	24 = X	25 = Y	26 = Z	

1. Romulus is the man we think founded Rome.
2. Toga is the white robe Romans wore.
3. Bronze is the metal Romans used for tools and weapons.

(continued on page 264)

Rome Solutions (continued)

Eternally Rome (continued from page 263)

4. Tiber is the river in Rome.

5. Republic is the kind of government in Ancient Rome. It allowed the citizens to participate in politics.

6. Roman numerals are the symbols that Romans used for numbers.

BONUS: Rome is nicknamed the Eternal City.

Mystery History (page 70)

You can see how the shaded boxes form the letter "F"—for Felix!

Colosseum	Spanish Steps	Trevi Fountain
Sistine Chapel	Big Ben	Statue of Liberty
Pantheon	Forum	Sphinx
"Ciao!"	tepees	Eiffel Tower
lira	chopsticks	knights

Chunk of the Colosseum (page 71)

This could be the missing piece of the Colosseum:

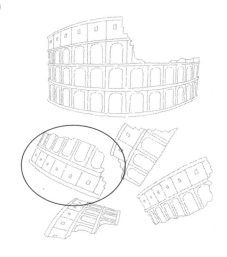

Cairo Solutions

Word from Egypt (pages 76–77)

¹C	²A	I	R	O		³L	I	O	⁴N
	R					A			I
⁵E	A	S	T		⁶R	E	A	L	
	B				G				E
⁷F	I	F	⁸T	Y	E			⁹P	
	C		R		S			H	
		¹⁰F	I	R	S	T		¹¹S	E	A
		A					R
¹²C	O	R	N				A
I		¹³G	I	Z	A		A
T		L				O
Y		¹⁴S	E	V	E	N		H

The bird on the Egyptian flag is the EAGLE.

Either Or (page 79)

1. Cairo has a hot climate.
2. Cairo is on the continent of Africa.
3. Cairo is a city, not a country, so this statement is false.
4. You might see a camel in Cairo.
5. Cairo is in Egypt, so someone who lives there would be called an Egyptian.
6. There is no right or wrong answer to this question, but Felix hopes that you said yes!

Solid Work (page 80)

You should have circled these three-dimensional items:

 Nairobi Solutions

The Detective (page 84)

1. Yes. Other languages are spoken in Kenya besides English and Swahili.
2. Yes. Zebras and elephants do live in Kenya. People like to watch them on safaris.
3. No. There is no snow skiing in Kenya. Kenya is on the equator, so it is too hot there for snow.
4. Yes. Kenya produces coffee, so you could see a truck carrying coffee beans.
5. No. Kenya is on the eastern coast of Africa, so it touches the ocean.

Pack Lightly (page 85)

Sophie won't need these things:

• *How to Speak Chinese* cassette because Chinese is not a common language in Nairobi
• *Great Things to See in Europe* because Nairobi is in Africa
• A *sled* because there is no snow in Nairobi
• *Gloves* and a *scarf* because it is not cold in Nairobi
• *The Felix Activity Book*, but Felix hopes she will take it anyway!

Can You Describe Kenya? (page 87)

There are many correct answers, but here are some possibilities:

ADJECTIVE	SYNONYM	ANTONYM	RHYMING WORD
sunny	bright	cloudy	funny
hot	scorching	cold	dot
flat	level	bumpy	hat
dry	arid	wet	fly
pretty	beautiful	ugly	city
fun	enjoyable	dull	run

Sunset Over Kenya (page 89)
There are many correct answers, but here are some possibilities:

	DIFFERENT SHADES OF THIS COLOR	THINGS THAT ARE THIS COLOR
BLACK	ebony	licorice, crows
BLUE	indigo, turquoise	oceans, blueberries
GREEN	emerald, olive	grass, cucumbers
PURPLE	violet, mauve	eggplants, lilacs
RED	crimson, scarlet	blood, cherries
WHITE	ivory, cream	snow, milk
YELLOW	gold, maize	corn, school buses

New York Solutions

The Apple's Core (pages 92-93)
Felix is directing Sophie to the **ice-skating rink** in Rockefeller Plaza.

BONUS: This activity is named "The Apple's Core" because New York City is nicknamed "the Big Apple," and this map shows midtown, which is like the "core" of the Big Apple.

When New York was Really New (page 94)

```
S  D  U  T  C  H  E  V  A  P
X  R  R  W  L  C  W  O  I  B
A  E  M  P  I  R  A  X  F  H
M  D  N  P  N  C  L  M  N  Z
S  U  D  E  N  G  L  I  S  H
T  T  V  S  O  D  O  K  E  U
E  G  A  M  S  T  E  E  M  D
R  W  Y  W  A  U  M  M  U  S
D  D  J  Y  C  E  X  P  R  O
A  L  G  O  N  Q  U  I  A  N
M  O  I  T  R  E  A  R  Y  Q
Z  H  U  D  S  T  H  E  K  S
```

Next Stop: Museum of Natural History (page 97)
The object that does not belong is the painting called the Mona Lisa. It is in the Louvre in Paris.

    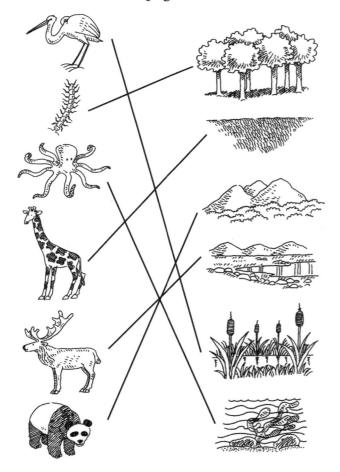

Environment Solutions

Follow Your Heart (page 102)

The living things are the ostrich, Sophie, the flower, the paramecium, and the apple tree. The living things with hearts are the ostrich and Sophie. The flower and apple tree are living plants, but plants do not have hearts. The paramecium is a living microorganism, but it also does not have a heart.

Take Me Home (page 103)

Polar Opposites (page 104)

POLAR WORD OR TERM	OPPOSITE	FACT
tip of the iceberg the North Pole	bottom of the iceberg the South Pole	Icebergs are often surrounded by fog. Penguins live in the South Pole; there are none in the North Pole.
winter	summer	In the polar regions, the sun shines all day and night in the summer.
small variety of animals	large variety of animals	Seals are the main food for polar bears.
white	black	Penguins are both.
water freezing to ice	ice melting to water	At its thickest, the ice in Antarctica is ten times taller than the Sears Tower in Chicago, the tallest building in America.

Ice Breaker (page 105)

The Temperate Society (page 107)

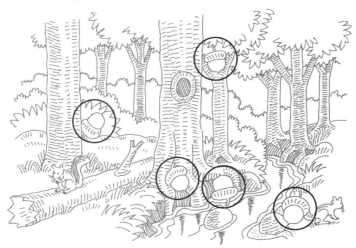

The five other acorns hidden throughout the book are on pages 3, 23, 46, 186, and 240.

Environment Solutions (continued)

Raking the Elaves (page 108)

The deciduous trees

1. oak
2. maple
3. elm

The evergreen trees

1. pine
2. fir
3. spruce

BONUS:

The activity is called "Raking the Elaves" because elaves rearranged spells leaves!

Life in the Rain Four-est (page 109)

The list that could be used to describe a tropical rain forest:
1. rainy, cold, green, filled with animals
2. rainy, hot, green, filled with animals
3. rainy, hot, green, without animals
4. dry, hot, green, filled with animals

The list with animals that all live in a tropical rain forest:
1. orangutans, toucans, tree frogs, harpy eagles
2. army ants, spider monkeys, sloths, penguins
3. army ants, bison, sloths, toucans
4. raccoons, spider monkeys, army ants, jaguars

The animals on these lists that don't live in a tropical rain forest are penguins, bison, and raccoons. Where do they live?

These continents have rain forests:
1. Africa
2. Asia
3. Australia
4. South America
5. North America—the woods of the northwest are often considered a rain forest

Layer Up (page 110)

Desert Crossings (page 111)

1.	d	e	s	e	r	t
2.	g	i	l	a		
		3.	h	u	m	p
	4.	c	a	c	t	u	s
5.	s	c	o	r	p	i	o	n
	6.	o	a	s	i	s

The **Sahara** in Africa is the world's largest desert.

Environment Solutions (continued)

Grasslands Are Always Greener (page 113)

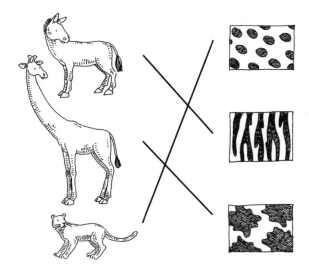

Mountain View (page 115)

woodchuck   mountain gorilla   golden eagle

High Altitude Jumble (page 116)

1. The **tree line** is the height on a mountain above which trees cannot grow because it is too windy and COLD.
2. When a VOLCANO erupts, lava shoots up, and steam and gas escape from the fissure in the Earth.

(continued on page 273)

High Altitude Jumble (continued from page 272)

3. The world's tallest mountain is EVEREST in the Himalayas in Asia.

4. There is less OXYGEN as you go higher up a mountain, making it more difficult to breathe.

5. A VULTURE is a bird that frequently looks in the mountains for animal carcasses to eat.

6. ALPINE is a word derived from the Alps mountain range that means "relating to high mountains."

Slippery When Wetland (page 117)

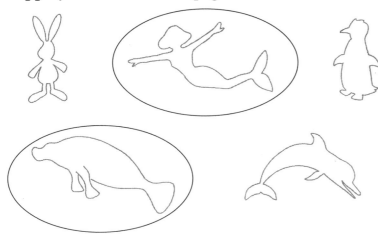

Deep, Very Deep (page 118)

These animals are in the pelagic habitat:
- sperm whale
- squid
- swordfish
- jellyfish

These animals are in the benthic habitat:
- sea anemone
- lobster

BONUS:
- The manta ray could be in either. It swims in the water but often buries itself in the sand of the ocean bottom.

Environment Solutions (continued)

Rain Forests of the Sea (page 119)
These are just some words that can be made from the letters CORAL REEF:

aloe	feel	of
are	feral	or
car	flare	oral
care	flee	ore
core	for	race
eel	free	rare
face	lace	real
far	leaf	reel
fare	leer	roar
fear	lore	role

 Stone Age Solutions

The First Firsts (page 125)
1. Walking upright (on two feet)
2. Using stone tools to get food
3. Speaking a language
4. Using fire
5. Living in huts
6. Using modified tools (such as blades and bone points)
7. Creating art (like sculpture and painting)
8. Wearing simple jewelry (beads)
9. Farming
10. Using animals (like dogs) as pets and helpers

Tool Time (page 128)

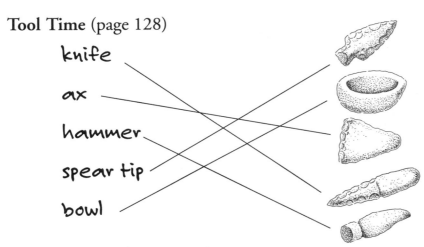

knife

ax

hammer

spear tip

bowl

Hot on the Trail (page 129)
The caveman is following a woolly mammoth.

 Ancient Greece Solutions

Thrill of Victory (page 132)

ROW 1: all discus throwers

ROW 2: all javelin throwers

ROW 3: all shot putters

DIAGONAL: all have black objects
(top left to bottom right)

COLUMN 1: all cast a shadow

COLUMN 2: all wear a tunic and rope belt

COLUMN 3: all make a fist with their left hand

DIAGONAL: all have their mouths open
(top right to bottom left)

Marathon Session (page 137)

1. The distance between your house and your mailbox is (probably) **shorter** than a marathon.

2. The distance between the Earth and the moon is **longer** than a marathon.

3. The distance that you can throw a ball is **shorter** than a marathon.

4. The distance between Greece and New York City is **longer** than a marathon.

5. The distance between the fingertips of your left and right hands when your arms are stretched out is **shorter** than a marathon.

BONUS: The distance between your house and your school could be either **longer** or **shorter** than a marathon. It depends on where you live.

Viking Solutions

Viking Truth (page 141)

1. True. Some historians think that Vikings came to North America before Christopher Columbus.
2. True. Leif Ericsson is the Viking captain who came and settled in North America.
3. True. Leif Ericsson's settlement was called Vinland, and it was most likely where Newfoundland, Canada, is today.
4. False. There is no evidence of a Viking settlement in Orlando, Florida.
5. True. Vikings did live in Scandinavia.
6. True. Norway, Sweden, and Denmark are countries in Scandinavia.
7. True. Vikings were also called Norsemen, or Northmen, because they were from northern Europe.
8. True. Vikings did settle Iceland.
9. False. Roofs of Viking houses were made of thatch, which is another word for straw.
10. False. Viking ships usually had only one big sail.

Ships Set Sail (page 145)

1. This ship is missing its sail.
2. This ship has a large hole in its side.
3. This ship has wheels.

Middle Ages Solutions

A Hard Day's Knight (pages 148–149)

These are the six sequences in which the stories can be read:

1 – 3 – 5
1 – 3 – 8
1 – 2 – 4 – 7 – 10
1 – 2 – 4 – 7 – 11
1 – 2 – 4 – 9
1 – 2 – 6

A Time of Growth (page 150)

1. Yes. The first large book was printed in Germany during the Renaissance.
2. Yes. The Mona Lisa was painted during the Renaissance by Leonardo da Vinci.
3. Yes. Cathedrals were built during the Renaissance in places such as Florence, Italy.
4. No. Railroads and automobiles were not invented until after the Renaissance.
5. Yes. Leonardo da Vinci had many interests and was very talented. In addition to painting, he also studied the way the human body works.

Woke Up on the Wrong Side of the Moat this Morning (page 151)

Felix can get across the moat in the following ways:

- Swing on the rope
- Row the boat
- Climb the tree
- Pole-vault with the stick

Of course, all of these activities could be dangerous, so neither Felix nor you should try them!

 Feudal Japan Solutions

Cops and Robbers (page 156)

You may disagree with some of these solutions. If so, write your reasons why!

WORD	GOOD	BAD	NEUTRAL
police officer	draw picture here		
vitamin C	draw picture here		
poison		draw picture here	
saying "please"	draw picture here		
stealing		draw picture here	
television			draw picture here

Feudal Japan Solutions (continued)

Japan by the Numbers (page 157)
1. 7 countries in the world have more people than Japan
2. 6 letters are written by Felix
3. 8 letters are in "Hokkaido"
4. 2 chopsticks are needed for one person to eat
5. 12 chopsticks are needed for the whole family (two for each person)
6. 8 languages in the world are more common than Japanese
7. 3 letters in the word "Tokyo" are not an "o"
8. 6 letters each are in each of the words "Honshu" and "Kyushu"
9. 5 places are visited by Felix besides feudal Japan (Stone Age, ancient Greece, time of the Vikings, Middle Ages, time of the Native Americans on the frontier)
10. 3 islands end with the letter "u" (Honshu, Kyushu, and Shikoku)
    60 is the total when you add these numbers together

Japan is the **60**th largest country in the world in area. This means that there are 59 countries with more land space than Japan.

Eye of the Storms (page 160)
1. A typhoon hits in the Pacific Ocean, near Japan.
2. A cyclone hits around the Indian Ocean.
3. A hurricane hits around the Atlantic Ocean.
4. A monsoon hits around the Indian Ocean and Asia.
5. A tornado, or twister, hits in the American midwest and in Africa.
6. A blizzard could hit anywhere there is snow!

A cyclone, hurricane, and typhoon are the same kind of storm, but they occur in different parts of the world.

Native American Solutions

Through the Woods (page 168)

Peaceful Land (page 169)
The **peace symbol** appears
in the stars.

 # Astronomy Solutions

Where in the Air Are You? (page 174)

1. You are in the layer where humans live.	troposphere
2. You are in the hottest layer of the atmosphere.	thermosphere
3. You are in an airplane.	stratosphere
4. You see a cloud fly by.	troposphere
5. You are in the layer where it is so close to space that there is no temperature.	exosphere
6. You are in one of the layers that is warmer at the bottom	troposphere, mesosphere

Everybody Line Up (page 179)

1. Which is shorter, a lunar eclipse or a solar eclipse?   solar
2. Which eclipse is visible during the day?   solar
3. What type of eclipse can be seen more often, a lunar or a solar?   lunar
4. Which eclipse is visible at night?   lunar
5. Can lunar eclipses and solar eclipses happen at the same time?   no

BONUS:

6. What would you call an eclipse where Sophie stands between Felix and the sun, casting a shadow on Felix?   A Felix eclipse!

Sunshine on My Shoulder (page 183)

Things that Go Twinkle in the Night (page 187)

CONSTELLATION ALPHABETIZED	ZODIAC SIGN?	CONSTELLATION ALPHABETIZED	ZODIAC SIGN?
Canis Major		Phoenix	
Cassiopeia		Pictor	
Cetus		Pisces	yes
Gemini	yes	Sagitta	
Hercules		Sagittarius	yes
Lacerta		Scorpius	yes
Microscopium		Scutum	
Monoceros		Telescopium	
Musca		Tucana	
Pavo		Vulpecula	

Astronomy Solutions (continued)

Not Your Average Meteor Shower (page 191)

Name that Moon (page 194)

1. The moon rotates very slowly.

   (Tortoise) or Tornado?

   A tortoise is a slow-moving type of turtle. A tornado is a fast-moving twist of wind.

2. The moon is covered with volcanoes.

   Glacier or (Lava?)

   A glacier is a piece of ice. Lava is extremely hot molten rock that comes out of volcanoes.

3. The moon is blue.

   (Cerulean) or Crimson?

   Cerulean is a shade of blue. Crimson is a shade of red.

4. The moon is made of rock.

   Coral or (Boulder?)

   Coral is an animal with a hard outer skeleton. A boulder is a big rock.

5. The moon is very small.

   (Miniscule) or Gargantuan?

   Miniscule means tiny. Gargantuan means huge.

6. You discovered the moon.

   someone else's name or your name?

   Either answer is acceptable, but how many people have moons named after them?

Reversed to Me Is Regular to You (page 199)

Mars Wordfinder (page 202)

```
M A S R O C E A N X E
T Y B A C O N M U W R
P L A N E T I A S A R
H W P I V D J K T R U
O A C M E R D Y A T S
B U R A C R E D R E T
O P A L B D I A F I Y
S E T S C O M E T R U
T S E A E I O U Y O P
M O R H W J S A I M N
V E N U S X R N S A N
O L Y M P U S M O N S
```

Words you may have found but should not have circled are *ocean, animals, star, war, comet, Venus,* and *bacon.*

Astronomy Solutions (continued)

Fast Planet (page 207)
These things move fast:

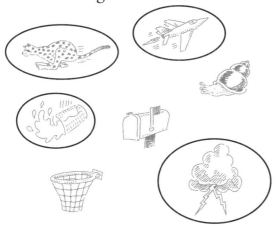

Do you think any of the things you circled move faster than Jupiter?
No, in this group, Jupiter is fastest.

The Naked Eye (page 210)
These can be seen with the naked eye:

Saturn   Earth's Moon   Blue Whale   clover

Tipping Permitted (page 214)

STATEMENT	URANUS ONLY	URANUS AND OTHER PLANETS
I am sideways.	✔	
I have rings.		✔
I have moons.		✔
I have fifteen moons.	✔	
I am named for a Roman god.		✔
I was discovered in 1781.	✔	

Marvelous Moon Math (page 215)

QUESTION	ANSWER
How many Earth hours equal one day on Uranus?	17
What day in March 1781 was Uranus discovered?	13
Which Voyager spacecraft took pictures of Uranus?	2
How many planets are closer to the sun than Uranus?	6
How many rings does Uranus have?	11
How many planets are bigger than Uranus?	2
How many Uranus moons did Herschel discover?	2

Rewrite the answers in the same order and calculate:

17 − 13 + 2 + 6 − 11 + 2 + 2 = $\boxed{5}$

Five of Uranus's moons were discovered on Earth.

The Big Switcheroo (page 222)

The item that cut in line is circled:

1. Sunday, Monday, Friday, Tuesday, Wednesday, Thursday, Saturday

2. a, b, c, d, e, f, g, h, i, j, k, l, n, m, o, p, q, r, s, t, u, v, w, x, y, z

3. June, July, August, September, November, October

4. 1998, 1997, 1999, 2000, 2001, 2002

5. nursery school, kindergarten, 2nd grade, 1st grade, 3rd grade

6. millimeter, centimeter, kilometer, meter

Rabbit Rerun Solutions

Living in the Past (page 226)

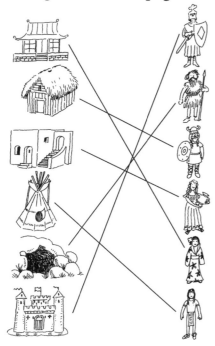

Hidden in Paris (page 227)

You should find the following items:

1. a red double-decker bus from London
2. a Colosseum from Rome
3. a Sphinx from Cairo
4. a shield and spear from Kenya
5. an Empire State Building from New York City.

Color the World Part 2 (page 228)

1. North America
2. South America
3. Europe
4. Africa
5. Asia
6. Australia
7. Antarctica

You could have colored each continent however you choose!

Then and Now (page 229)

THEN — NOW

church or synagogue
horse
computer
stone
telephone
fire pit
car
Parthenon
oven
pen, ink, and scroll
smoke signals
hammer

1. horse and car: modes of transportation
2. stone and hammer: used to pound something
3. fire pit and oven: used for cooking
4. Parthenon and church or synagogue: used as places of worship
5. pen, ink, and scroll and computer: used to write
6. smoke signals and telephone: used to communicate long distance

World According to Felix (page 232)

1. Felix visits 3 continents: Europe, Africa, and North America.

2. Felix didn't see 4 continents: South America, Asia, Australia, and Antarctica.

3. London, Paris, Rome, Cairo, and Nairobi are the capitals of their countries.

Capitals Quiz (page 234)

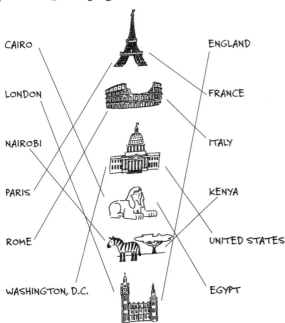

Over Yonder (page 235)

1. New York City is farther away from London than Cairo.

2. Paris is the closest to London.

3. Cairo and Nairobi are in Africa.

4. Nairobi is farther south than Cairo.

5. Paris is between London and Rome.

6. Rome is farther away from Paris than London.

7. London, Paris, and Rome are in Europe.

8. Rome is the closest to Cairo.

9. When Felix was in Paris, he could only visit one other city by car. That city is Rome.

10. One city is west of London. That city is New York City.

Rabbit Rerun Solutions (continued)

Holiday Shuffle (page 239)

HALLOWEEN	WORD AFTER CHANGE IS MADE
Change the "LL" to an "N."	HANOWEEN
Change the "EE" to an "A."	HANOWAN
Change the "O" to the vowel that comes after "O."	HANUWAN
Change the "H" to a "K."	KANUWAN
Change the second "N" to an "H."	KANUWAH
Move the "K" to where the "W" is, and remove the "W."	ANUKAH
Put a "CH" back in front.	CHANUKAH

THANKSGIVING	WORD AFTER CHANGE IS MADE
Take out all the "G"s.	THANKSIVIN
Take out all the "I"s.	THANKSVN
There is 1 vowel left. Add 2 more of the same at the end.	THANKSVNAA
Change the "T" to a "C."	CHANKSVNAA
Change the "H" to a "W."	CWANKSVNAA
Replace the "SVN" with a "Z."	CWANKZAA
Move the "K" to where the "C" is, and remove the "C."	KWANZAA

Connecting the Celebrations (page 240)

Christmas in China
paper lantern

Kwanzaa
kinara

Christmas in Mexico
piñata

Christmas in Sweden
crown of evergreen leaves

Chanukah
dreidel

Christmas in the Netherlands
white horse

All I Want for Christmas Is a Biome (page 242)

1. England — desert or ~~temperate forest?~~

2. Sweden — ~~temperate forest~~ or polar tundra?

3. The Netherlands — ~~temperate forest~~ or grasslands?

4. Germany — tropical rain forest or ~~temperate forest?~~

5. Italy — taiga or ~~mountain?~~

6. Russia — ~~taiga~~ or ocean?

7. China — ~~desert~~ or polar tundra?

8. Australia — taiga or ~~desert?~~

9. Mexico — ocean or ~~desert?~~

10. United States — ~~mountain~~ or taiga?

Call Me a Rat, Snake, or Pig—I Don't Mind (page 243)

DESCRIPTION	ANIMAL	YEARS
Looks like a bigger, uglier mouse	rat	1948, 1960, 1972, 1984, 1996
Large bull with big horns	ox	1949, 1961, 1973, 1985, 1997
Orange-and-black striped wild cat	tiger	1950, 1962, 1974, 1986, 1998
Felix!	rabbit (hare)	1951, 1963, 1975, 1987, 1999*
Fictional, fire-breathing lizard	dragon	1952, 1964, 1976, 1988, 2000
Slithering reptile with no legs	snake (serpent)	1953, 1965, 1977, 1989, 2001
Every cowboy and cowgirl rode one	horse	1954, 1966, 1978, 1990, 2002
White, woolly farm animal, says "baa"	sheep (ram, goat)	1955, 1967, 1979, 1991, 2003
Small, chattering ape with tail	monkey	1956, 1968, 1980, 1992, 2004
Male chicken, says "cock-a-doodle-doo"	rooster	1957, 1969, 1981, 1993, 2005
Common pet, "man's best friend"	dog	1958, 1970, 1982, 1994, 2006
Pudgy, pink farm animal, says "oink"	pig	1959, 1971, 1983, 1995, 2007

Don't be offended if someone calls you a rat, snake, or pig. It just may be the truth!

* This book is published in the Year of the Rabbit—Felix's year!

Rabbit Rerun Solutions (continued)

Your Dark Side (page 244)

When the sun is directly overhead, Felix's shadow is between his feet.
When the sun is low in the sky, his shadow is much longer than he is.
When the sun is high, his shadow is shorter than he is.

Chain, Chain, Chain of Food (page 247)
The food chains:
1. grass, antelope, lion
2. worm, chicken, human
3. krill, blue whale, killer whale
4. plant plankton, clam, fish, bear
5. leaf, grasshopper, frog, snake, owl
6. tree leaves, caterpillar, sparrow, eagle, vulture

Superlative Ecosystems (page 248)
1. Sophie is the **smartest** girl in her class.
2. The owl is the biggest bird in the world. **false**
3. What do you think is the **scariest** movie ever made?
4. Felix is the **most polite** rabbit of them all.
5. Everyone likes chocolate. **no superlative**
6. Who has the **most** money?

Asteroids, Comets, and Meteorites, Oh My! (page 249)

1. I am made of dirty ice.	comet
2. I am one of many that orbit the sun in a belt.	asteroid
3. Before I landed on Earth I was called a meteor.	meteorite
4. I have a tail.	comet
5. My name means "starlike."	asteroid
6. I am a star.	none

Cosmic Disturbance (page 250)

The planets, from biggest to smallest:

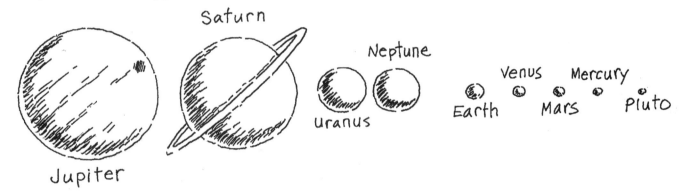

An End Is a Beginning (page 253)

There are many right answers, but here are a few:

Europa	asteroid, asteroid belt, Andromeda, Armstrong (Neil)
Saturn	Neptune, nebula, North Star, nova
Scutum	moon, meteor, Mars, Milky Way
Venus	Saturn, supernova, solar system
Neptune	Earth, eclipse, Europa
Io	orbit, Orion, observatory

Subject Index (activity pages only; **bold** means the word is defined)

Subject Index (continued)

Skills Index

Web Sites

Holidays

achristmas.com (Christmas)

members.aol.com/yaechicago/chanukah.htm (Chanukah)

tbwt.com (Kwanzaa)

www.4hanukkah.com (Chanukah)

www.christmas.com (Christmas)

www.festivals.com (festivals)

www.jcn18.com (Jewish Communication Network)

www.kenaz.com/notes/chinese_animal.htm (Chinese New Year)

www.melanet.com (Kwanzaa)

www.ort.org (Chanukah)

www.peders.com (Christmas in Scandanavia)

Time

www.china-contact.com (Chinese calendar)

www.erols.com/bcccsbs/chincal.htm (Chinese calendar)

www.scoutnet.net.au/chinese/horoscope.html (Chinese zodiac)

www.webindia.com/emperorclock (pendulum clock)

Environment

library.advanced.org/11353/text/ecosystems.htm (ecosystems)

members.aol.com/bowermanb/ecosystems.html (ecosystems/biomes)

pc65.frontier.osrhe.edu/hs/science/biome1.htm (biomes)

science.cc.uwf.edu/sh/Curr/foodchain/foodchain.htm (food chains)

seamonkey.ed.asu.edu/~hixson/index/spiders.html (spiders)

ucs.byu.edu/bioag/aghort/aghort100/climates.htm (climates)

www.angelfire.com/hi/biomelinks/ (biomes)

www.csun.edu/~csc24235/ecosys.html (ecosystems)

www.discovery.com (general nature)

www.envirolink.org/earthday/history.html (Earth Day)

www.fs.fed.us/colorimagemap/images/app1.html (climates)

www.libby.org/plummer/powerpt/weather1/tsld008.htm (levels of atmosphere) www.ozkidz.gil.com.au (endangered species)

www.panda.org/kids/wildlife/idxtrpmn.htm (biomes)

www.polarbearsalive.org/ (polar bears)

www.richmond.edu/~ed344/97/biomes/biomes.html (biomes)

www.sedl.org/scimath/pasopartners/spiders/background.html (spiders)

www.si.edu/organiza/offices/sites/exhibit/manatees.htm (manatees)

www.themesh.com/un.html (Earth Day)

www.the-north-pole.com (North Pole)

www.ups.edu/biology/museum/worldbiomes.html (biomes)

Astronomy

www.cotf.edu (NASA classroom of the future)

www.exploratorium.edu/ronh/weight/ (weight on other planets)

www.mars.sgi.com/ (Mars missions)

wwwflag.wr.usgs.gov/ (United States Geological Survey) [note: there is no point
   in address between "www" and "flag"!]

Miscellaneous

www.biography.com (biographies)

www.education-world.com (education)

www.encyclopedia.com (encylopedia)

www.s9.com (biographies)

www.windows.umich.edu/cgi-bin/tour.cgi/long.button.map

Multimedia

Microsoft Bookshelf 98

World Book Multimedia Encyclopedia, The, World Book Inc., 1998

Sites active as of this printing. We are not recommending any other sites advertised on or linked to these sites.

Contest: Create an Activity for Felix's Next Book!

Felix loves making activities for you. How would you like to make one for him?

In fact, if you win the contest, he will publish it in his next activity book!

It's so easy to enter:
1. Get permission from your parent or guardian.
2. Complete the form on this page or fill in each field in an e-mail message. E-mail entries must include a statement of approval written by the parent or guardian.
3. Send it in!

E-mail (sent no later than March 1, 2001): *felix@abbeville.com*

Postal mail (postmarked no later than March 1, 2001):
Felix Activity Contest
c/o Abbeville Press
22 Cortlandt Street
New York, NY 10007

Name_____
Street Address_____
City_____
State_____
ZIP code_____
Phone_____
E-mail_____
Age_____
Name of Parent or Guardian_____
Approval Signature of Parent or Guardian _____
On the back of this sheet (or within your e-mail message), write your activity on any subject.
Illustration is not required, although you may include it if necessary.

No purchase necessary. All entries become property of Abbeville Press. By submitting an entry you are granting permission for reproduction without compensation at any time. Felix and friends will choose one activity as the winner. The winner will be notified by phone and in writing by May 1, 2001. The winner's name will appear in the next book, publication of which is subject to change.

Letter to Felix 1
Write a letter to Felix about your last visit to your friend's house or apartment.

Dear Felix,

Letter to Felix 2

Write a letter to Felix about your last visit to a museum.

Dear Felix,

Letter to Felix 3

Write a letter to Felix about your last visit to someplace scary.

Dear Felix,

Letter to Felix 4
Write a letter to Felix about your last visit to another city.

Dear Felix,

Letter to Felix 5

Write a letter to Felix about your last visit to another country (if you haven't been to another country, pick one, read about it, then write a letter).

Dear Felix,

Letter to Felix 6
Write a letter to Felix about your last visit to a bookstore or a library.

Dear Felix,